Community Experiences

Reading and Communication for Civics

McGraw-Hill

Lynda Terrill

Community Experiences, 1st Edition

Published by McGraw-Hill ESL/ELT, a business unit of The McGraw-Hill Companies, Inc. 1221 Avenue of the Americas, New York, NY 10020. Copyright © 2005 by The McGraw-Hill Companies, Inc. All rights reserved. No part of this publication may be reproduced or distributed in any form or by any means, or stored in a database or retrieval system, without the prior written consent of The McGraw-Hill Companies, Inc., including, but not limited to, in any network or other electronic storage or transmission, or broadcast for distance learning.

3 4 5 6 7 8 9 QPD 9 8 7

ISBN: 0-07-287075-3

Editorial director: *Tina B. Carver*
Executive editor: *Erik Gundersen*
Developmental editors: *Jean Bernard, Louis Carrillo*
Production managers: *Juanita Thompson, Mary Rose Bollwage*
Interior designer: *Wanda España, Wee Design Group*
Cover designer: *Wanda España, Wee Design Group*
Illustration: *Tina Widzbor*

The McGraw·Hill Companies

McGraw-Hill

Acknowledgements

The publisher and author would like to thank the following individuals who reviewed *Community Experiences* during the development of the project and whose comments and suggestions were invaluable in its creation.

* Scott Chiverton, *Glenn County Office of Education*, Orland, CA

* Karen Dennis, *Centennial Education Center*, Santa Ana College, Santa Ana, CA

* Peggy Doherty, *CASAS*, Alameda, CA

* Bophany Huot, *City College of San Francisco*, San Francisco, CA

* Laura Martin, *Adult Learning Resource Center*, Des Plaines, IL

* Patricia Mooney-Gonzalez, *New York State Department of Adult Education*, Albany, NY

* Gilda Rubio-Festa, *Central Piedmont Community College*, Charlotte, NC

* Kathleen Santopietro Weddel, *Northern Colorado Literacy Resource Center*, Longmont, CO

* Dan Wann, *English Works in Indiana*, Santa Claus, IN

* Yelena I. Zimon, *EL Civics Education Program Coordinator*, Fremont Adult School, Fremont, CA

Lynda thanks her husband, Tom, for making room for one more project and her daughter, Sarah, for the research. She thanks her editor and friend, Jean Bernard, for keeping the vision clear. Lynda thanks her friends and colleagues at the National Center for ESL Literacy Education and the Arlington Education and Employment Program. Most of all, Lynda thanks the adult learners who have taught her so much about the American Dream and who continue to help strengthen our neighborhoods, our communities, and our country.

Community Experiences

Community Experiences introduces students to concepts that are fundamental to participating in American society while it provides multiple opportunities for them to practice and develop new language skills in a communicative setting.

ENGLISH CIVICS

CHAPTER **2**

LEARNING FOCUS

Content:
- Types of community participation in the United States

Reading Skills:
- Using a dictionary or glossary to learn new words
- Finding supporting details in a paragraph
- Reading for the main idea

Civics Activities:
- Voting
- Making a map
- Exploring a town or neighborhood
- Visiting a community resource and obtaining information
- Organizing community information

Getting to Know the Community

1 Think Ahead

Discuss these questions with a partner or small group.

- ★ What is happening in these pictures?
- ★ What do you know about participating or in your native country?
- ★ What more do you want to know abou community?

1 Learning Focus identifies the content, reading skills, and language skills at a glance for lesson-planning purposes.

2 Contemporary and historical photographs stimulate student interest.

2 Read About It

A. Read along or listen to the passage. Circle the words you want to remember.

B. Read Paragraph 1 or Paragraph 2 again.

C. Use a dictionary or the glossary on pages 93–96 to learn about new words. Write new words and their definitions in your vocabulary notebook.

Participating in Community Life

The term *community participation* includes all the ways people express ideas, learn, have fun, help out, and make changes in their communities. Going to the library, having a picnic at the local park, or discussing a neighborhood problem are all ways to participate in the community.

1   The tradition of civic and community participation comes from several sources. The First Amendment of the U.S. Constitution gives citizens freedom of religion, freedom of speech, freedom of the press, the right to peaceful assembly, and the right to ask the government to change. Two hundred years ago when this Amendment was signed, this law gave more freedom to talk, write, and take action than people in other countries had. Many cultural and religious groups who immigrated to this land brought cooperative ideas with them. Also, in the rural areas where many Americans lived, it was necessary for people to help their neighbors. Settlers helped each other build houses or barns and harvest crops.

2   Community participation continues today. Americans debate about schools, transportation, or whom they want for president. In fact, Americans debate about almost everything! Citizens can vote for the people and ideas they support, but people also participate in other ways. Many people visit libraries and parks and recycle their garbage. Some people join community, school, political, or cultural organizations. Other people volunteer at clinics, schools, and shelters. Some immigrants use their language skills to translate at local hospitals. Others donate food and help build houses for the homeless.

3 Think Ahead activity activates prior knowledge and helps the teacher gauge student readiness to tackle the topic.

4 **The language of the readings** is appropriate for the linguistic level of the student and is also cognitively demanding. Readings include description, exposition, and narration.

5 **Audio icon** indicates that the reading is included in the audio program.

6 **Numbering of paragraphs** in the readings helps teachers and students locate information efficiently.

D. Finish the sentences with words from the paragraph you read.

PARAGRAPH 1

1. Freedom of religion, speech, and the press are protected by the _____ _____ to the U.S. Constitution.

2. The First Amendment also gives citizens the rights to peaceful _____ and to ask the _____ to change.

3. In rural areas, settlers helped their _____ by building houses or barns.

PARAGRAPH 2

1. Americans often _____ in their communities by debating about things such as schools, transportation, and whom they want for president.

2. Other people participate in their communities by going to _____ and by recycling their garbage.

3. Today, many people help their neighbors by volunteering at clinics, schools, and _____.

E. Work with a partner who read the other paragraph. Ask and answer questions so that you both understand the information in both paragraphs.

EXAMPLES: What paragraph did you read? What did you learn? What new vocabulary did you learn? What is the main idea of the paragraph?

F. In small groups, talk about your native countries. Give examples of community participation in your native countries.

EXAMPLES: How do people express their opinions in your native country? In what ways do people help each other in your native country?

Did You Know?

Margaret Mead was a famous anthropologist who had many opinions on the cultures she studied as well as on her own culture. She once said, "Never doubt that a small group of thoughtful, committed citizens can change the world. Indeed, it's the only thing that ever has."

Getting to Know the Community ★ 9

---

3 **Brainstorm**

A. List some more ways people participate in t...

go to school meetings

_____

_____

B. Think of more reasons why people want to communities.

get important information

_____

_____

_____

C. Make a chart like this for your class. Write down the languages students speak in the left column. Write the number of speakers of each language in the middle. Write the purposes why students speak their languages on the right.

Languages	Number of Speakers	Purposes
Arabic	3	to talk to friends and family at a holiday celebration at the park
Spanish	12	to discuss news events in our countries
English	–	to complain to the landlord about a broken window

10 ★ Chapter 2

7 **Red type** cues students that the word is included in the glossary at the back of the book.

8 **Frequent repetition of vocabulary and ideas** helps ensure comprehension. Students are asked to practice new vocabulary, identify speakers, identify main ideas and details, and evaluate information given in a reading.

9 **Did you know?** presents a short, high-interest reading along with a compelling graphic that allow students to expand their knowledge of the chapter topic.

4 Plan

A. Work in small groups to plan for participating with your classmates in three community experiences. Follow these steps.

1. Discuss the things you already know about your community. How have you participated in community life? What language did you use? Make a list to present to the class.

   EXAMPLE: Maria went to a farmer's market. She spoke English.

2. Look through the remaining chapters in this book (see p. vii). Which topics do you think are most important? Discuss your choices with your group.

B. As a class, vote for the community experiences in this book that you would like to have. Write your three top choices (1, 2, and 3) on a slip of paper. One classmate can collect the votes and write the totals on the board. Which topics are the winners?

Congratulations! In English, you have debated with your classmates, expressed your opinions, and voted in an election. You are ready to participate in the community outside your classroom. Good luck!

5 Community Experience: Exploring Your Neighborhood

A. Explore your town or the neighborhood near your school.

★ Group 1: Make a map with street names, bus or train stops, police and fire stations, schools, hospitals, and other important public buildings.

★ Group 2: Make a list of businesses in the area, including shops, restaurants, and services.

★ Group 3: Go to the library, a government office, or a community center. Pick up all the free schedules, papers, and newsletters about the community like sports team schedules, clinic hours, and holidays. Organize the information in a notebook or box.

B. Make a list of useful questions, answers, and polite conversation words to use when you explore your community.

   EXAMPLE: Excuse me, can you tell me . . .

C. Share your information with the class.

---

10 Brainstorm activities use prompts and graphic organizers to help students apply the chapter ideas to their lives outside of class.

6 Reflect

Choose one of the topics below. Write about it in your journal, or talk about it with the class.

1. In Chapter 2, you worked with partners and groups inside and outside of class. Do you think this is a good way to learn English? Why or why not?

2. Do you think that one person, for example, Martin Luther King, Jr., or Mother Teresa, can change the world? Explain.

3. Do you think that September 11, 2001, has changed the way people participate in their communities? Why or why not?

7 Assess

What did you learn about community participation in the United States? What would you still like to learn? Fill in the chart with your own ideas and information.

I learned:	New words and phrases I want to remember:	I would like to learn more about:

Resources ★★★★★★★★★★★★★★★★★★

★ **The First Amendment, the Bill of Rights, and the Constitution**
Read pages 85–86 in the back of this book, invite someone from the League of Women Voters to talk to your class, or go online to ***www.lwv.org***.

★ **Community activities**
Many communities have Websites. Go to ***www.google.com*** and type your city (or county) and state into the search box. For example:

| New York New York | Search |

★ **Find a map of your neighborhood or city**
In addition to the library or the local government office, you can find maps at many stores or go online to ***www.mapquest.com***.

---

11 Plan and Community Experience encourage students to use what they have learned outside the classroom, building confidence and skills.

12 Reflect and Assess activities allow students to integrate, reflect on, and record what they have learned.

Contents

Scope and Sequence

Chapter	Content
CHAPTER 1 **Civics in American Life**	★ History of civic participation in the United States
CHAPTER 2 **Getting to Know the Community**	★ Types of community participation in the United States
CHAPTER 3 **Going to School**	★ History of education in the United States
CHAPTER 4 **Using the Public Library**	★ History of public libraries in the United States
CHAPTER 5 **Finding Out About Local Government**	★ Federal, state, and local government in the United States
CHAPTER 6 **Understanding the Legal System**	★ The United States legal system
CHAPTER 7 **Finding Help in an Emergency**	★ Emergency assistance
CHAPTER 8 **Accessing Health Care**	★ Types of health care and health insurance programs in the United States
CHAPTER 9 **Workers' Rights and Responsibilities**	★ The rights and responsibilities of workers in the United States
CHAPTER 10 **Finding Good Places to Live**	★ Places to live in the United States
CHAPTER 11 **Enjoying Local Parks and Recreation**	★ Local parks and recreation services
CHAPTER 12 **Helping Out With the Environment**	★ Protection of the natural environment
CHAPTER 13 **Living Together in a Multicultural Land**	★ Life in a multicultural country
CHAPTER 14 **Making a Difference in the Community**	★ Community volunteers

Reading Skills ★	**Civics Activities** ★
★ Using a dictionary or glossary to learn new words ★ Finding the main idea of a paragraph	★ Identifying interesting topics in American history ★ Finding and sharing information on a topic in American history
★ Using a dictionary or glossary to learn new words ★ Finding supporting details in a paragraph ★ Reading for the main idea	★ Voting ★ Exploring a town or neighborhood ★ Visiting a community and obtaining information
★ Using a dictionary or glossary to learn new words ★ Finding specific details to complete sentences ★ Understanding time phrases	★ Finding information about education programs in the community ★ Visiting a school in the community and obtaining information ★ Inviting a guest educator to class and interviewing him or her ★ Summarizing educational information
★ Using a dictionary or glossary to learn new words ★ Reading for specific details to complete sentences	★ Interviewing partners about their library habits ★ Planning a group visit to a local library ★ Drawing a map ★ Visiting a local library and obtaining information
★ Using a dictionary or glossary to learn new words ★ Scanning for specific information ★ Interpreting numbers for reading	★ Identifying types of local government services ★ Finding out about local government services ★ Comparing government services in the U.S. with those in another country
★ Using a dictionary or glossary to learn new words ★ Reading for specific information ★ Learning the history of words	★ Inviting a law enforcement official to class and interviewing her or him ★ Visiting a local courthouse or police station and obtaining information
★ Using a dictionary or glossary to learn new words ★ Reading for specific information ★ Interpreting the words and meaning of a song	★ Getting and sharing information about a community's emergency services ★ Analyzing safety problems in a school
★ Using a dictionary or glossary to learn new words ★ Taking notes	★ Identifying medical problems ★ Finding and sharing information about medical problems
★ Using a dictionary or glossary to learn new words ★ Reading for specific information	★ Planning a panel discussion about workers' rights and responsibilities ★ Inviting employers and employees to speak to the class ★ Recording the panel discussion and sharing it with another class
★ Using a dictionary or glossary to learn new words ★ Reading for specific information	★ Identifying housing in the community ★ Finding out about rules for landlords and tenants ★ Learning about the Fair Housing Act of 1968 ★ Finding out about getting financial help with housing
★ Using a dictionary or glossary to learn new words ★ Scanning for specific details ★ Categorizing information	★ Planning a visit to a local recreation facility ★ Learning about the rules of a local recreation facility ★ Visiting a recreation facility and obtaining information
★ Using a dictionary or glossary to learn new words ★ Identifying the main idea ★ Identifying specific details	★ Finding information to start a recycling center at school ★ Planning a class or family garden ★ Learning about natural habitats ★ Researching a community environmental problem
★ Using a dictionary or glossary to learn new words ★ Reading for specific information	★ Finding out where languages of the world are spoken ★ Getting information about future cultural activities in the community ★ Sharing information about a local cultural event ★ Hosting a class or school multicultural event
★ Using a dictionary or glossary to learn new words ★ Identifying the main idea ★ Identifying specific details	★ Getting information about volunteering ★ Analyzing availability and skills for volunteering

Dedication

Community Experiences is dedicated to the adult immigrant learners I taught at the Arlington Education and Employment Program in Arlington, Virginia.

Community Experiences is dedicated to:

* The Vietnamese woman who told me what it was like to be a young girl in Da Nang during the Vietnam War. She shared Christmas with my family and cried when my father died.

* The Moroccan man who didn't write in French, Arabic, or English. He never smiled until the class went to the park to learn about the community: sports, laughs, and a picnic. Who knew he was a great athlete? After the volleyball game, he never stopped smiling.

* The Salvadoran woman who taught me to make pupusas in my own kitchen.

* The Bolivian man—a kid, really—who gave me my first tape of Bolivian music. He's dead now. I hope he is resting in peace.

* The Somali women who could speak only a little English, but who were able to tell me about war, death, and survival.

* The Afghan young man—brilliant, everyone's friend, the peacemaker— I've wanted to talk to him since September 11.

* To all those classes who went to the Capitol, the Washington Monument, the Smithsonian, the National Zoo, the Cherry Blossom Festival, the park, the store, the fair, the Halloween parade, Arlington Cemetery, the Metro, the Bolivian night club, my house, and the Blue Ridge Mountains.

This book is dedicated to you and the thousands of other immigrant learners who are enriching the United States.

Lynda Terrill

To the Teacher

Welcome to *Community Experiences.*

This book has three interrelated purposes for students: to read and communicate in English, to learn American history that is interesting and relevant to their lives, and to learn how and when to be active participants in their communities. That may seem to be a tall order for one book, but in fact, many adult English language learners are already working hard on these three purposes.

In *Community Experiences,* my goal is to give teachers and learners a framework to help with this complex and important learning and to provide information or access to information that will be of use to them. The text is based on ideas of learner-centered and project-based education because those have been effective in my own teaching and learning. Respect for the strengths, experiences, needs, and goals of adult English language learners is the underlying principle of the book and the impetus for the eclectic, high-interest readings and activities. The activity processes and information will prove helpful not only in learning English but also in life outside the classroom.

The first two chapters provide the cultural and historic context for civic participation in the United States and a rationale for participating in one's community. The other twelve chapters place these ideas in familiar contexts such as school, health, and work, and some slightly less common contexts such as recreation, environmental issues, and volunteering. After the initial two chapters, the class and teacher can decide in what order they will progress through the chapters.

In *Community Experiences,* some of the options for activities occur outside the realm of what the teacher or student may perceive as traditional education, so it is important to know that similar activities have been successfully completed with learners at this low- intermediate level as well as at both lower and higher levels. For teachers who want more specific information about such topics as learner needs assessment, learner-centered approaches, project-based learning, and working with multilevel classes, two- and four-page ERIC Digests (funded by the Office of Vocational and Adult Education, United States Department of Education) are available for downloading from www.cal.org/ncle/digests/ .

In each chapter, project work is supported by a process that leads learners from an introductory discussion and reading through thinking, planning, and researching to achieving focused learning goals inside or outside the classroom. Each chapter includes the following seven sections:

1. **Think Ahead** uses guiding questions and picture prompts to introduce the chapter topic. These questions serve as a quick check of learners' knowledge and interest in the topic so the teacher can adapt the activities to meet the needs of the class. The prompts have been chosen to activate learner interest and to demonstrate the breadth of civic and community participation possible across topics as diverse as the signers of the U.S. Constitution and community garbage recycling.

2. **Read About It** gives learners the opportunity to listen to and read information about the topic at hand. Individualized vocabulary acquisition is encouraged, and highlighted content words are explained in a glossary. Proper names with a number after them are explained in the Notes. Comprehension activities give learners a chance to gather new content knowledge while improving reading skills.

3. **Brainstorm** moves the learners a step closer from reading history or statistics to their own lives and experience. In this activity the whole group brainstorms answers to two prompts such as "What kinds of emergencies happen in your community?" and "List the people and organizations you can contact in an emergency." Because brainstorming is a popular technique in school, business, and the community, this activity may help learners to be effective when they participate in community groups.

4. **Plan** gives step-by-step instructions on how learners can think about, research, and organize the individual, group, or class activity that has been decided upon. In this section, learners always encounter the question "Where can you find information?" and pertinent answers to guide the research. The purpose of this section is to give individuals, partners, or groups the chance to work together in English to find information or decide on a process that will help them to learn information that is important to them.

5. **Community Experience** is the core of the book. Some chapters culminate with activities outside the class—going to the library or park or visiting a courtroom—with classmates, alone, or with friends and family. In other chapters, the community experience could be inviting a panel in to talk to the class, or researching topics of interest and then sharing the information. In all chapters—whether in conversations, posters, or videos—there is a great deal of information sharing. So whenever community learning or participation occurs, natural, content-rich communication is also going on.

6. **Reflect** offers students an opportunity to think about issues and ideas that have arisen during the chapter. Three questions for journal writing or further conversation are posed. The questions typically expand or extend the issues that have been discussed and are useful for serving learners in a multilevel class.

7. **Assess** gives individuals a chance to informally review what they learned in the chapter, declare what words and phrases they want to remember, and think about what more they would like to learn about the chapter topic.

Other Features

Call-out box: Adjacent to the readings, this box defines, explains, or amplifies a language, historical, or cultural point from the reading.

Did You Know?: Each chapter contains a high interest photograph and caption about American history or culture related to the chapter topic. For example, Chapter 1 shows the famous photo of the Greensboro, North Carolina, lunch counter sit-in. The photo anchors the idea of civic participation in learners' minds while it shares an important piece of American culture.

Where can you find information?: Adjacent to the Plan section, this box gives specific tips on where to find information.

Resources: At the end of the chapter, this section lists books, videos, and Websites related to the chapter focus. This section gives some basic hints about how to find books in the library and how to do a simple search on the Internet. This final element brings each chapter back to the goal of assisting adult learners in learning English and finding information in their own communities and in their own lives.

Components

The complete Community Experiences program includes the following components:
* Student Book   ISBN: 0-07-287075-3
* Teacher's Manual   ISBN: 0-07-287076-1
* Audiocassette   ISBN: 0-07-287077-x
* Audio CD   ISBN: 0-07-299206-9

The teacher's manual includes an answer key for exercises and a test for each of the chapters. The audiocassette and audio CD include recordings of all of the reading selections in the Student Book. Audio icons ⌒ throughout the book indicate places at which teachers may choose to play the audiocassette or audio CD in class.

Lynda Terrill

To the Student

Welcome to *Community Experiences*.

There are three goals for this book:

- to help you read and communicate in English
- to offer you interesting and useful information about American history and culture
- to help you learn how and when to participate in your community

This book asks you to read, think, and write about the history, government, and culture of the United States. The book asks you to compare the United States with your native country and share ideas with other people in your class. *Community Experiences* asks you to talk and work with your classmates because that's a good way to learn English and a good way to learn about other ideas and cultures. Learning in class also helps you know how to talk and work with people in your community.

The first chapter of the book, "Civics in American Life," tells the history of civic participation in the United States. The second chapter of the book, "Getting to Know the Community," talks about how the law encourages civic participation and gives examples of ways people participate or help out in their communities.

In Chapter 2, you can vote about the kinds of community experience you want. Do you want to get a library card? Learn about the legal system? Find out how to join a sports team? The other 12 chapters ask you to read, write, talk, plan, and do activities that you choose.

Community Experiences tells you important and interesting facts about the United States. The book gives you advice about finding information and talking to people in your community at the same time you are learning more English.

I think the United States is a good place to live because of the laws that encourage freedom and equality. I think it is a good country because of all the native peoples and immigrants—voluntary and involuntary—who have come here. Since the beginning, these many peoples have helped make a strong country. As you are learning English and participating in your community, you too are helping build our country's future.

Lynda Terrill

CHAPTER 1

LEARNING FOCUS

Content:

★ History of civic participation in the United States

Reading Skills:

★ Using a dictionary or glossary to learn new words

★ Finding the main idea of a paragraph

Civics Activities:

★ Identifying interesting topics in American history

★ Finding and sharing information on a topic in American history

Civics in American Life

1 Think Ahead

Discuss these questions with a partner or small group.

★ What is happening in these pictures?
★ Who do you think the people are?
★ What more do you want to know about them?

A. Read or listen to the passage. Circle the words you want to remember.

B. Choose one of the paragraphs to read on your own.

C. Use a dictionary or the glossary on pages 91–94 to learn about new words. The words in red are all in the glossary. Write new words and their definitions in your vocabulary notebook.

Civic Participation in the United States

> **Civic participation** is the idea that all people—not just kings, political and religious leaders, or rich people—can and should have a voice and be active in their government. This idea has had a strong influence on the history, society, and government of the United States.

Native Americans

1   In many Native American groups in North America, people discussed and solved problems by talking together in a meeting. A person could give his or her opinion about important community problems. This example of civic participation began long before the European settlers came to North America.

Pilgrims

2   The Pilgrims were English immigrants who came to North America in 1620. They were looking for religious freedom. Before the Pilgrims got off their ship, the *Mayflower,* the men signed the Mayflower Compact. It was a document that explained how they were going to govern their new colony in North America.

Slavery

3   Slavery of Africans and their descendants began in the Jamestown colony in 1619. Slavery was legal in some Southern states until 1865. Many men, women, and children who fought against slavery were slaves themselves. They faced danger and sometimes died when they tried to obtain their freedom by going north on the Underground Railroad. Many other people helped by speaking and writing against slavery.

Women and Migrant Workers

4   For most of the history of the United States, American women were not able to vote. They worked together for the right to vote. They finally won this right in 1920. In the 1960s, Cesar Chavez was a leader of Mexican-American migrant farm workers in California. He organized a boycott to help workers receive better working conditions and wages.

D. Choose one of the paragraphs to read again.

E. Answer the questions about the paragraph you read.

PARAGRAPH NUMBER _____

1. Who is this paragraph about?

   _____

2. What time in history is the paragraph about?

   _____

3. What does the paragraph describe?

   _____

4. Why is this important?

   _____

F. Talk with classmates who read the same paragraph you read. Compare your answers so you all understand the information.

G. Form new groups. Every group needs to have one person from each of the groups in the "puzzle" on the right. Tell the group about the information you learned.

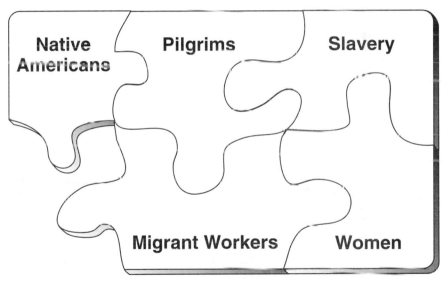

Native Americans

Pilgrims

Slavery

Migrant Workers

Women

Did You Know ?

After slavery ended, some basic civil rights were still denied African-Americans, especially in the South. Special laws called "Jim Crow" laws required separate drinking fountains, restaurants, and schools for blacks and whites. Although this segregation was made illegal in 1954, it took 10–15 years for most of the unequal treatment to stop. This photo shows a peaceful sit-in for equal service at a lunch counter in Greensboro, North Carolina.

3 Brainstorm

A. List some more examples of civic participation in the United States.

voting for public officials

_____

_____

_____

B. List more examples of civic participation in another country you know.

organizing a school in . . .

_____

_____

_____

C. Discuss these questions with a partner first, then with a small group, and finally with the whole class.

1. What information do you need so you can participate in your community?

2. What problems need to be solved in your community?

3. How can you help your community?

D. Write your class's answers to the questions above on large paper to post on the wall, or type the answers on a computer so everyone can have a copy.

4 Plan

A. Look over the list below. Check (✓) the topics that you would like to learn more about.

_____ Native Americans who lived near where you live now

_____ The Pilgrims or other early settlers

_____ The Revolutionary War

_____ Slavery in the United States

_____ The fight for women's voting rights

_____ The civil rights movement of the 1950s and 1960s

_____ Cesar Chavez and migrant farmworkers

_____ Civic participation in your native country

_____ *your idea*

B. From the topics you checked, choose the one that you are most interested in. Get together with another classmate who chose the same topic. Write a list of at least five questions.

EXAMPLE: When did the first slaves come to America?

1. _____

2. _____

3. _____

4. _____

5. _____

5 Community Experience: Finding Information

A. Write down important facts and where you found the information (books, Websites, etc.).

Where can you find information?

★ Ask your teacher for books or papers to read.

★ Look on the Internet.

★ Go to the school or public library. Ask a reference librarian for help.

Facts	Resources
first slaves in Jamestown in 1619	*A Synopsis of American History, page 5*

B. Share your information with the class. You can write one or two paragraphs, make a drawing or poster, talk to the class, or even play music or show a video.

6 Reflect

Choose one of the topics below. Write about it in your journal, or talk about it with the class.

1. What did you think about the activities in this chapter? Was it helpful for you to work with a partner or in small groups? Why or why not?

2. Do you think that civic participation is as important now as it was in the past? Is it important for you? Explain.

3. In the early days of the United States, only white men were able to vote. Why do you think this changed?

7 Assess

What did you learn about civic participation in the United States? What would you still like to learn? Fill in the chart with your own ideas and information.

I learned:	New words and phrases I want to remember:	I would like to learn more about:

Resources ★ ★ ★ ★ ★ ★ ★ ★ ★ ★ ★ ★ ★ ★ ★ ★ ★ ★

★ **United States history**
Go to the public library and search in the 970 section for books such as the series

> *A History of the United States* by Joy Hakim. (1998).
> **New York: Oxford University Press** (elementary and
> middle school levels)

★ **Civil rights movement of the 1950s and 1960s**
There are many books, videos, CDs, and audiocassettes about the civil rights movement at the library. You can also look on the Internet at the Library of Congress Website called "From Slavery to Civil Rights" at ***www.memory.loc.gov/learn/features/civilrights/flash.html***.

★ **Local history**
Go online to ***www.google.com***. In the search box, type the name of your city (or county), your state, and the word "history." For example:

Los Angeles California history Search

Getting to Know the Community

1 Think Ahead

Discuss these questions with a partner or small group.

- ★ What is happening in these pictures?
- ★ What do you know about participating in the community here or in your native country?
- ★ What more do you want to know about participating in the community?

A. Read along or listen to the passage. Circle the words you want to remember.

B. Read Paragraph 1 or Paragraph 2 again.

C. Use a dictionary or the glossary on pages 91–94 to learn about new words. Write new words and their definitions in your vocabulary notebook.

Participating in Community Life

The term *community participation* includes all the ways people express ideas, learn, have fun, help out, and make changes in their communities. Going to the library, having a picnic at the local park, or discussing a neighborhood problem are all ways to participate in the community.

1   The tradition of civic and community participation comes from several sources. The First Amendment of the U.S. Constitution gives citizens freedom of religion, freedom of speech, freedom of the press, the right to peaceful assembly, and the right to ask the government to change. Two hundred years ago when this Amendment was signed, this law gave more freedom to talk, write, and take action than people in other countries had. Many cultural and religious groups who immigrated to this land brought cooperative ideas with them. Also, in the rural areas where many Americans lived, it was necessary for people to help their neighbors. Settlers helped each other build houses or barns and harvest crops.

2   Community participation continues today. Americans debate about schools, transportation, or whom they want for president. In fact, Americans debate about almost everything! Citizens can vote for the people and ideas they support, but people also participate in other ways. Many people visit libraries and parks and recycle their garbage. Some people join community, school, political, or cultural organizations. Other people volunteer at clinics, schools, and shelters. Some immigrants use their language skills to translate at local hospitals. Others donate food and help build houses for the homeless.

D. Finish the sentences with words from the paragraph you read.

PARAGRAPH 1

1. Freedom of religion, speech, and the press are protected by the _____ _____ to the U.S. Constitution.

2. The First Amendment also gives citizens the rights to peaceful _____ and to ask the _____ to change.

3. In rural areas, settlers helped their _____ by building houses or barns.

PARAGRAPH 2

1. Americans often _____ in their communities by debating about things such as schools, transportation, and whom they want for president.

2. Other people participate in their communities by going to _____ and by recycling their garbage.

3. Today, many people help their neighbors by volunteering at clinics, schools, and _____.

E. Work with a partner who read the other paragraph. Ask and answer questions so that you both understand the information in both paragaphs.

EXAMPLES: What paragraph did you read? What did you learn? What new vocabulary did you learn? What is the main idea of the paragraph?

F. In small groups, talk about your native countries. Give examples of community participation in your native countries.

EXAMPLES: How do people express their opinions in your native country? In what ways do people help each other in your native country?

Did You Know ?

Margaret Mead was a famous anthropologist who had many opinions on the cultures she studied as well as on her own culture. She once said, "Never doubt that a small group of thoughtful, committed citizens can change the world. Indeed, it's the only thing that ever has."

A. List some more ways people participate in their local communities.

go to school meetings

_____

_____

_____

B. Think of more reasons why people want to participate in their communities.

get important information

_____

_____

_____

C. Make a chart like this for your class. Write down the languages students speak in the left column. Write the number of speakers of each language in the middle. Write the purposes why students speak their languages on the right.

Languages	Number of Speakers	Purposes
Arabic	*3*	*to talk to friends and family at a holiday celebration at the park*
Spanish	*12*	*to discuss news events in our countries*
English	*–*	*to complain to the landlord about a broken window*

4 Plan

A. Work in small groups to plan for participating with your classmates in three community experiences. Follow these steps.

1. Discuss the things you already know about your community. How have you participated in community life? What language did you use? Make a list to present to the class.

   EXAMPLE: Maria went to a farmer's market. She spoke English.

2. Look through the remaining chapters in this book (see p. vii). Which topics do you think are most important? Discuss your choices with your group.

B. As a class, vote for the community experiences in this book that you would like to have. Write your three top choices (1, 2, and 3) on a slip of paper. One classmate can collect the votes and write the totals on the board. Which topics are the winners?

Congratulations! In English, you have debated with your classmates, expressed your opinions, and voted in an election. You are ready to participate in the community outside your classroom. Good luck!

5 Community Experience: Exploring Your Neighborhood

A. Explore your town or the neighborhood near your school.

★ Group 1: Make a map with street names, bus or train stops, police and fire stations, schools, hospitals, and other important public buildings.

★ Group 2: Make a list of businesses in the area, including shops, restaurants, and services.

★ Group 3: Go to the library, a government office, or a community center. Pick up all the free schedules, papers, and newsletters about the community like sports team schedules, clinic hours, and holidays. Organize the information in a notebook or box.

B. Make a list of useful questions, answers, and polite conversation words to use when you explore your community.

   EXAMPLE: Excuse me, can you tell me . . .

C. Share your information with the class.

6 Reflect ★

Choose one of the topics below. Write about it in your journal, or talk about it with the class.

1. In Chapter 2, you worked with partners and groups inside and outside of class. Do you think this is a good way to learn English? Why or why not?

2. Do you think that one person, for example, Martin Luther King, Jr., or Mother Teresa, can change the world? Explain.

3. Do you think that September 11, 2001, has changed the way people participate in their communities? Why or why not?

7 Assess ★

What did you learn about community participation in the United States? What would you still like to learn? Fill in the chart with your own ideas and information.

I learned:	New words and phrases I want to remember:	I would like to learn more about:

Resources ★ ★ ★ ★ ★ ★ ★ ★ ★ ★ ★ ★ ★ ★ ★

★ **The First Amendment, the Bill of Rights, and the Constitution**
Read pages 85–86 in the back of this book, invite someone from the League of Women Voters to talk to your class, or go online to **www.lwv.org**.

★ **Community activities**
Many communities have Websites. Go to **www.google.com** and type your city (or county) and state into the search box. For example:

New York New York **Search**

★ **Find a map of your neighborhood or city**
In addition to the library or the local government office, you can find maps at many stores or go online to **www.mapquest.com**.

Going to School

LEARNING FOCUS

Content:

★ History of education in the United States

Reading Skills:

★ Using a dictionary or glossary to learn new words

★ Finding specific details to complete sentences

★ Understanding time phrases

Civics Activities:

★ Finding information about educational programs in the community

★ Visiting a school in the community and obtaining information

★ Inviting a guest educator to class and interviewing him or her

★ Summarizing educational information

1 Think Ahead

Discuss these questions with a partner or small group of your classmates:

★ What is happening in these pictures?

★ How are schools in your native country different from schools in the United States?

★ What more do you want to know about schools in the United States?

A. Read or listen to the passage. Circle the words you want to remember.

B. Use a dictionary or the glossary on pages 91–94 to learn about new words. Write new words and their definitions in your vocabulary notebook.

Education in the United States

> The time phrase *in the 1800s* tells the reader about an event or condition that was true from 1800 to 1900, the nineteenth century. *In the early 1900s* refers to the first part of the twentieth century, from 1900 to about 1930.

1   Schools and education are important in every community in the United States. Education has always been important to this country, but it has varied in different places and different times. Boston was the busiest port city in North America in the 1600s. Many boys and some girls went to school there.

2   Harvard College began near Boston, Massachusetts, in 1636 and is the country's oldest university. Sometimes pioneer children were taught basic reading, writing, and arithmetic by their parents. During slavery times, access to education was denied to slaves. In fact, in some southern states, it was illegal to teach a slave to read and write.

3   In the 1800s and early 1900s, many immigrant children were not able to go to school because they worked in factories, in mines, or on farms. Until the 1930s, school schedules for children of farming families were based on the farming seasons. Now all children are required to attend school until they are 16 years old. Most children go to free public schools, but some go to private schools or are home-schooled. Children attend school for approximately 180 days a year. Children usually go to school from September to June.

C. Finish the sentences with words from the reading.

1. The oldest university in the United States is in _____.

2. Pioneer parents sometimes taught their children basic _____ , _____ , and _____.

3. It was _____ to teach a slave to read and write in some southern states.

4. In the early part of the last century, many _____ children could not go to school because they had to _____.

5. Now all children must _____ school.

D. Answer the questions below about yourself.

EXAMPLE: Did you go to school in your native country or another country? Yes, I did. I studied in my country, El Salvador.

1. Did you go to school in your native country or another country? How long?

_____

2. What was your favorite subject in school?

_____

3. Have you gone to school in the United States?

_____

4. If yes, what subjects did you study?

_____

5. What subject do you want to learn more about now?

_____

E. Now talk with a classmate about his or her school experiences. Ask the questions in Activity D.

EXAMPLE: Tell me about school in your country. Did you go to school in your country?

Did You Know ?

Horace Mann (1796–1859) grew up in a poor farming family in Massachusetts. He only went to school three months a year. Later he became a lawyer, politician, and college president. He fought for free non-religious public education for all children. Many public schools in the U.S. are named after Horace Mann.

3 Brainstorm ★

A. List some questions you would like to ask about the schools in your community.

How much does it cost? _____

_____

_____

_____

B. List at least three reasons for adults to go to school.

to learn computer skills _____

_____

_____

_____

_____

4 Plan ★

A. Work in small groups to plan one of these projects.

★ Group 1: Find out how and when you can visit your child's school to observe his or her class. You will need to call for an appointment. Work with the group to think of good questions to ask.

★ Group 2: Find out about educational programs for adults in your community (in addition to English). Write out some questions to ask about schedules, fees, and starting dates. Plan to visit or call the program to ask your questions.

★ Group 3: Make an appointment to talk to the administrator of your adult education program. Make a list of questions you would like to ask.

★ Group 4: You choose. For example, you could find out about the colleges and universities in your area or visit a community college.

B. Plan to invite an educator to visit your class. Follow these steps.

1. Talk together, then vote to decide who you want to invite to class: for example, a teacher or principal from the public schools, a teacher from a vocational school, or someone from a college or university.

2. Select someone in your class to call your guest. Be sure to have all the information ready, such as the time and place your class meets, directions, and parking or public transportation information.

3. Prepare a list of questions you would like the person to answer.

Where can you find information?

★ Check the local newspaper for advertisements.

★ Look on the Internet.

★ Call the reference librarian at the public library.

★ Look in the yellow pages of your telephone book under "schools."

A. Follow your plan in Activity 4. Then fill in answers to the questions in the chart below.

Where did you go?	
Where is the school or program located?	
Who did you talk to?	
What did you learn about the students?	
What did you learn about the program?	

B. Take notes on your guest speaker's visit. Then write out answers to the questions you prepared and fill in the information in the chart below.

Guest speaker's name and title	
School or program	
Interesting information	1. 2. 3.

6 Reflect

Choose one of the topics below. Write about it in your journal, or talk about it with the class.

1. In what ways are schools in your native country and in the United States the same? In what ways are they different? From what you've seen so far, which system do you prefer? Why?

2. Do you think going to school is always necessary for a person to be successful? Why or why not?

3. Some people think that the schools in the United States are not good because the children don't always listen to or obey their teachers. Other people think the schools are great because they teach children how to think for themselves. What do you think?

7 Assess

What did you learn about schools in the United States and in your community? What would you still like to learn? Fill in the chart with your own ideas and information.

I learned:	New words and phrases I want to remember:	I would like to learn more about:

Resources ★ ★ ★ ★ ★ ★ ★ ★ ★ ★ ★ ★ ★ ★ ★

★ History of schools in the United States
Look in the 370.973, 372, and 973.2 sections of the public library. One book you might find is

A School Album by Peter and Connie Roop.
(1999). Des Plaines: Heinemann Library
(elementary school level)

★ Helping your child in school
Call your local school and ask for a conference. Ask for an interpreter if you need English help.

★ Adult education, English, and GED classes near you
Call America's Literacy Directory at 1-800-228-8813 or look on the Internet at _www.literacydirectory.org_.

CHAPTER **4**

LEARNING FOCUS

Content:

* History of public libraries in the United States

Reading Skills:

* Using a dictionary or glossary to learn new words
* Reading for specific details to complete sentences

Civics Activities:

* Interviewing partners about their library habits
* Planning a group visit to a local library
* Drawing a map
* Visiting a local library and obtaining information

Using the Public Library

1 Think Ahead

Discuss these questions with a partner or small group.

* What is happening in these pictures?
* What do you know about public libraries here or in your native country?
* What more do you want to know about libraries in the United States?

A. Read or listen to the passage. Circle the words you want to remember.

B. Use a dictionary or the glossary on pages 91–94 to learn about new words. Write new words and their definitions in your vocabulary notebook.

Use *such as* to introduce one or more examples.

For example, you can say: I enjoy fruits *such as* oranges, lemons, and limes.

Public Libraries in the United States

1   In the United States, libraries are important community resources. In the late 1800s, a rich immigrant from Scotland named Andrew Carnegie gave money to start free public libraries. Now, almost all communities in the United States have free public libraries.

Andrew Carnegie, 1835–1919

2   Libraries have books, magazines, audiocassettes, videocassettes, CDs, DVDs, and even computer games. Many libraries also have computers with Internet access for everyone to use. When people visit the library, librarians help them find information they need about any topic.

3   Library cards are free. With a library card, a person can borrow books and other materials to take home. At most public libraries, people can check out books for two or three weeks. Most libraries

★ ★ **LIBRARY CARD** ★ ★

01234 56789

I agree to be responsible for all library materials checked out on this card.

PUBLIC LIBRARY

also have special activities, such as reading to young children and helping people fill out income tax forms.

C. Finish the sentences with words from the reading.

1. _____ are important community resources in the United States.

2. _____ gave money to start free public libraries.

3. You can find books, magazines, audiocassettes, _____,
   CDs, DVDs, and computer games at a public library.

4. _____ help people find information they need.

5. With a library card, a person can _____ books to
   take home.

D. Write answers to the following questions.

1. Is there a library in your community? Have you visited it? If no,
   where is the closest library? _____

2. Do you have a library card? If yes, what materials have you checked
   out? _____

   _____

E. Now ask a partner these questions. Check (✔) the questions when your
partner says *yes*.

_____ Have you visited a library?

_____ Do you have a library card?

_____ Have you checked something out of the library?

F. Work with the whole class to answer the following questions.

1. How many people in your class have a library card? _____

2. How many people in your class have checked out books or other
   materials from the library? _____

3. How many people in your class would like to get a library card?
   _____

Did You Know ?

Abraham Lincoln became president in 1861 and was the president during the Civil War. When Lincoln was a poor young farmer, he walked many miles to borrow books to read. He stayed up late and read by the fire.

3 Brainstorm

A. Make a list of reasons why people use the library.

borrow books _____

_____

_____

_____

B. Think of reasons why it is difficult for some people to use the library.

don't have a car _____

_____

_____

_____

4 Plan

A. Work in small groups to plan a trip to the library. Here is one way to organize the groups:

★ Group 1: Learn how people can get library cards and get registration forms for the class to fill out.

★ Group 2: Find out about transportation. Draw a map that shows how to get to the library. Find out about buses or trains that stop near the library.

★ Group 3: Find out the rules of the library. How many books or videos can a person borrow? Is there a late fine for overdue books?

★ Group 4: Make a class plan. When and where will the class meet? How many people will go in cars? How many will walk? How many will take the bus?

B. Share your information with the class.

C. Invite a librarian to visit your class. Decide what questions you will ask.

Where can you find information?

★ Call the library.
★ Look on the Internet.
★ Ask a friend.

5 Community Experience: At the Library

A. Work alone, with a partner, or in a small group to find the following places and things in the library. Check (✔) each one you find.

_____ circulation desk	_____ books in other languages
_____ reference desk	_____ computers
_____ audio-visual department	_____ bathrooms
_____ children's room	_____ public telephones
_____ magazines	_____ newspapers

B. Write three sentences about the places and things you found.

EXAMPLE: The bathrooms are near the circulation desk.

1. _____

2. _____

3. _____

C. Apply for a library card at the circulation desk. If you can, check out a book, CD, DVD, or video from the library. Then answer these questions.

1. What did you have to do to get your library card?

   _____

2. What is the name of the book, CD, DVD, or video you borrowed?

   _____

3. Why did you choose it?

   _____

4. When is the due date?

   _____

D. Take notes on the librarian's visit to your class. Be sure to ask questions. Write a short paragraph about the library to give to the students in another class. Write a thank-you note for the librarian.

6 Reflect

Choose one of the topics below. Write about it in your journal, or talk about it with the class.

See page 85 for more information on the First Amendment.

1. What did you think about the visit to the library? Will you go again? Why or why not? Who will you take with you? Why?

2. Do you think public libraries are important for people and communities? Why or why not?

3. The First Amendment gives us freedom of speech. Is this freedom connected to free public libraries? Explain.

7 Assess

What did you learn about libraries in the United States and in your community? What would you still like to learn? Fill in the chart with your own ideas and information.

I learned:	New words and phrases I want to remember:	I would like to learn more about:

Resources

★ **Andrew Carnegie**
   Look in the biography section of the public library. Two books you might find are

   Andrew Carnegie: Builder of Libraries by Charmon Simon (1997).
   New York: Children's Press. (elementary school level)

   Andrew Carnegie: Steel King and Friend to Libraries
   by Zachary Kent. (1999). Springfield NJ: Enslow
   Publishers (middle school level)

   Also look on the Internet at *Andrew Carnegie: A Tribute from the Carnegie Library of Pittsburgh,*
   www.clpgh.org/exhibit/carnegie.html.

★ **Your local public library**
   Visit or call the public library or information number for the local government, or go online to **www.google.com**. In the search box, type the name of your city (or county) and state and the words *public library*. For example:

   | Chicago Illinois public library | Search

CHAPTER 5

Content:

★ Federal, state, and local government in the United States

Reading Skills:

★ Using a dictionary or glossary to learn new words

★ Scanning for specific information

★ Interpreting numbers in a reading

Civics Activities:

★ Identifying types of local government services

★ Finding out about local government services

★ Comparing government services in the U.S. with those in another country

Finding Out About Local Government

1 Think Ahead ★

Discuss these questions with a partner or small group.

★ What is happening in this picture?
★ Who do you think the people are?
★ Why do you think they are in this office?

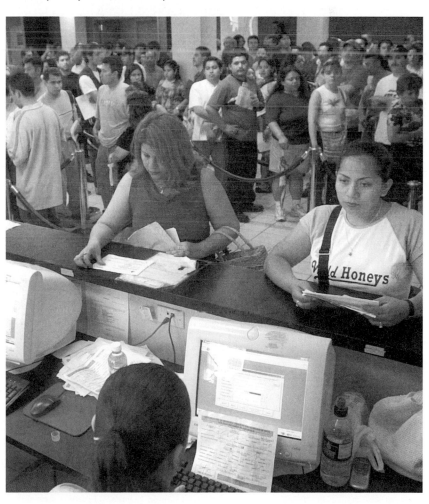

A. Read or listen to the passage. Circle the words you want to remember.

B. Use a dictionary or the glossary on pages 91–94 to learn about new words. Write new words and their definitions in your vocabulary notebook.

Levels of Government in the United States

Jurisdiction comes from the Latin word *iūrisdictīo,* which means "the administration of justice."

1   The United States has many levels of government. In addition to one federal government in Washington, D.C., there are governments for each of the 50 states, 4 territories, and 2 commonwealths. There are 3,066 counties in the United States. The county with the smallest population in the U.S. is Loving County, Texas, with a population of 67. The county with the largest population is Los Angeles County, California, with a population of 9,519,338.* There are separate governments for cities, towns, townships, and other jurisdictions. There are even regional governments made up of groups of local governments.

2   Some jurisdictions, such as New York City, are governed by mayors elected by the local citizens. Some places are governed by city or county boards. All of these governments must follow three general rules: They cannot contradict the United States Constitution; they must provide services to the people in their jurisdictions; and they must protect the rights and safety of citizens, permanent residents, visitors, and undocumented persons.

*U.S. Census, 2000

C. Scan the reading for the numbers that go with each word or phrase.

1. __1__ federal government

2. _____ states

3. _____ territories

4. _____ counties

5. _____ Loving County, Texas

6. _____ Los Angeles County, California

D. Explain to a partner what each number means.

EXAMPLE: There is only one federal government in the United States.

E. Fill in the chart with information about yourself. Where do you live?

state	I live in _____
county	
city or town	
other	

F. Share your information with a partner. Then ask each other these questions.

1. How long have you lived in _____?

2. Do you like living in _____?

3. What is your favorite thing about living in _____ _____?

4. What is difficult about living in _____?

Did You Know ?

The Navajo are the largest group of Native Americans. There are approximately 300,000 Navajo in the United States. About half of the Navajo live on the Navajo Reservation, which is outside the jurisdiction of any U.S. federal or state government. The reservation is about 25,000 square miles within the states of Arizona, New Mexico, and Utah. See the map on pages 88–89. The Navajo Nation has its own elected government with both local and tribal level elections.

3 Brainstorm ★

A. What do you like about living in your community? List as many good things as you can.

safe places for kids to play _____

_____

_____

_____

B. What is difficult about living in your community? List the problems.

high rents _____

_____

_____

_____

4 Plan ★

A. Circle the type of information about local government you need most. Ask your teacher about terms you do not understand.

child care	recreation programs
civic associations	rental assistance
drivers' licenses	small business licenses
food stamps	summer programs for children
garbage collection	Women, Infants, and Children Program (WIC)
pest control	other _____
property tax	

B. Form groups with people who need the same type of information you do. Work together with your group to decide what questions you want to ask. Use the question words in the box to help you get started.

> What . . . ?   When . . . ?   Where . . . ?   How . . . ?   Who . . . ?
>
> How much . . . ?   How often . . . ?   What if . . . ?   Why . . . ?

C. Decide how, where, and when you will find answers to your questions.

1. Will you work alone, with a partner, or with your group?

2. How will you get the information you need? (go to the library, use the Internet, go to a government office, call on the telephone)

3. When will you get the information? (during class, after school, at night, on the weekend)

5 Community Experience: Exploring Local Government

A. Find the answers to your questions and take notes. Write down the most important facts and ideas you want to share with your classmates.

Where can you find information?

★ Look in the government section of the telephone book.

★ Check your local government Website on the Internet.

★ Call the reference librarian at the public library.

★ Look at a government information brochure.

QUESTIONS	NOTES

B. Share the information you learned with your class or school. Write a paragraph, make a poster, or give an oral presentation to the class.

6 Reflect ★

Choose one of the topics below. Write about it in your journal, or talk about it with the class.

1. Compare the town or city you live in now with where you lived in your native country. In what ways are they the same? In what ways are they different?

2. Did you like writing the questions to ask a government worker? Did you feel confident when you asked the questions? Why or why not?

3. Do you think that government services such as schools, libraries, and food assistance should be available to undocumented immigrants? Why or why not?

7 Assess ★

What did you learn about local government in the United States and in your community? What would you still like to learn? Fill in the chart with your own ideas and information.

I learned:	New words and phrases I want to remember:	I would like to learn more about:

Resources ★ ★ ★ ★ ★ ★ ★ ★ ★ ★ ★ ★ ★ ★ ★ ★

★ **Local government in general**
Look in the 320.8 section of the public library. A book you might find is

> *Local Government* by Ernestine Giesecke. (2000).
> **Chicago: Heinemann Library** (elementary school level)

★ **Your local government**
Go to **_www.google.com_** on the Internet. Type in your town (or county), state, and the word *government*. For example:

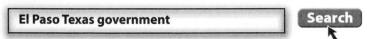

★ **Local history**
Call or visit your local public library. Most libraries have special sections with books, papers, and photographs about the local area.

Understanding the Legal System

1 Think Ahead

Discuss these questions with a partner or small group.

★ What is happening in these pictures?

★ What happens when someone breaks a law in your native country?

★ What do you want to know about the legal system in the United States? Write 3–4 questions.

A. Read or listen to the passage. Circle the words you want to remember.

B. Use a dictionary or the glossary on pages 91–94 to learn about new words. Write new words and their definitions in your vocabulary notebook.

The Legal System of the United States

Many legal terms, such as *legal, jury,* and *judicial,* come from Latin. The word *justice* comes from Latin *justitia,* which means "rights." You can learn the history of words in a good English dictionary.

1   The legal system of the United States is based on the Constitution. Even though the U.S. Constitution was written over 200 years ago and is only about 20 pages long, it is the supreme law of the land. All national, state, and local laws must follow the general rules of the Constitution and the Bill of Rights. For example, one of the rules says that people have rights against unreasonable searches and seizures.* This means that police officers are not allowed to enter a person's house or car without the written permission of a judge unless a crime is taking place or there is probable cause that the person committed a crime.

2   The legal system is very large and complex, but it has one goal—to provide justice for all. It consists of thousands of laws, law enforcement officers, courts, and judges. The system serves the people and the community in many ways. Laws help protect people's rights and keep them safe from criminals. The laws of a community also set the rules for things such as starting a business, getting married, getting divorced, and settling an argument with neighbors.

*For more information, read the Bill of Rights on pages 85–86.

C. Finish the sentences with words from the reading.

1. The main topic is the _____ _____ of the United States.

2. The _____ is the foundation of all the laws in the country.

3. The police must have written permission from a _____ before they can enter a person's house or car.

4. The purpose of the legal system is to _____ _____ for all.

D. Answer the questions about yourself.

1. Do you know where the local courthouse is? If yes, where?

   _____

2. Do you know where you can call if you have a question about local rules? For example, where can you call if you want to know how to get a marriage license?

   _____

3. Do you know where to go in your community if you need help translating and understanding laws or rules? If yes, where?

   _____

E. Now ask a small group of classmates the questions in Activity D. Then complete the sentences below and share your information with the whole class.

1. The courthouse is _____ .

2. Good places to call for information about local rules are _____ and _____ .

3. A good place to go for help in translating and understanding laws or rules is _____ .

Did You Know ?

In 1919, Congress passed the Eighteenth Amendment to the Constitution, which outlawed the selling of alcohol—beer, wine, and hard liquor. This law was very hard to enforce. Many people didn't like the law. They said it restricted their personal choice. The law was repealed by the Twenty-first Amendment in 1933, and alcohol could be sold again.

3 Brainstorm

A. List several things that are important to know about the legal system.

how to get help if you don't understand a law

_____

_____

_____

B. Think of reasons why it is sometimes difficult for people to get the information they need.

don't have a computer

_____

_____

_____

4 Plan

A. Work in small groups to plan a field trip to a courthouse or to your local police station.

★ Group 1: Find out where the courthouse or police station is and when and if your class can visit. Also find out when and if you can visit alone or with your friends or family.

★ Group 2: Make a list of suggestions about what to bring (like notebooks and pencils). Call to find out the rules for what you can and cannot bring with you.

★ Group 3: Prepare and bring a list of questions you want answered or information you want to learn.

★ Group 4: Make a class plan. When and where will the class meet? How many people will go in cars? How many will walk? How many will take the bus?

B. Plan to invite a police officer, a lawyer, or a judge to visit your class. Follow these steps.

1. Talk together, then vote for the person you want to invite to class: a lawyer to talk about immigration laws or civil rights, a judge to talk about courts in the United States, or a police officer to talk about keeping safe.

2. Prepare a list of questions you would like your guest to answer.

Where can you find information?

★ Look on the Internet.

★ Call the reference librarian at the public library.

★ Check the government section of the telephone book.

---

5 Community Experience: At the Courthouse or Police Station

A. Follow your plan for visiting the courthouse or police station. Then answer the questions in the chart below.

Where did you go?	
What is the address and phone number?	
How did you get there?	
Who did you talk to?	
What did you learn about the legal system?	1. 2.

B. Listen carefully to your guest speaker's presentation. Then complete the information in the chart below.

Name and title	
Important ideas	1. 2.
Interesting facts and statistics	1. 2.

6 Reflect

Choose one of the topics below. Write about it in your journal, or talk about it with the class.

1. What did you think about the visit to the courthouse or police station? Will you go again? Why or why not?

2. Do you think the legal system should protect and support undocumented immigrants as much as it does documented immigrants and citizens? Why or why not?

3. Since the terrorist attacks of September 11, 2001, the government now has more legal rights to search and detain people they think may be terrorists. Do you think this is a good idea? Why or why not?

7 Assess

What did you learn about the legal system in the United States and in your community? What would you still like to learn? Fill in the chart with your own ideas and information.

I learned:	New words and phrases I want to remember:	I would like to learn more about:

Resources ★ ★ ★ ★ ★ ★ ★ ★ ★ ★ ★ ★ ★ ★ ★ ★

★ **The United States Constitution**
Look in the 342.73–342.573 section of the public library. A book you might find is

The U.S. Constitution and You by Syl Sobel. (2001).
Hauppauge, NY. Barron's Education Series (elementary school level)

★ **Immigrants' civil rights**
Check the American Civil Liberties Website at
www.aclu.org/ImmigrantsRights/ImmigrantsRightsMain.cfm.

★ **Your local courts or police**
Visit or call the public library or call the information number for the local government.
Search the Internet using ***www.google.com.*** In the search box, type the name of your city (or county) and state and the words *courts, police,* or *city government.* For example:

| Miami Florida courts | Search |

Finding Help in an Emergency

1 Think Ahead

Discuss these questions with a partner or small group.

★ What is happening in these pictures?

★ How can people get emergency help here or in your native country?

★ What more do you want to know about finding emergency help?

A. Read or listen to the passage. Circle the words you want to remember.

B. Use a dictionary or the glossary on pages 91–94 to learn about new words. Write new words and their definitions in your vocabulary notebook.

Emergency Assistance

The word *aid* can be used as a noun, verb, or adjective. The verb means "help" or "give assistance." Do not confuse this word with *AIDS*, which stands for the condition *Acquired Immune Deficiency Syndrome.*

See page 95 for more information on Benjamin Franklin.

1   Since colonial times, professional and volunteer emergency aid workers have helped in their local communities and the country. For example, the first paid fire department began in Boston, Massachusetts, in the 1680s, and Benjamin Franklin[1] organized the first volunteer fire department in 1735 in Philadelphia, Pennsylvania. In the early days of the country, emergency medical help was often provided by women who knew how to help in childbirth, with trauma injuries, and with common illnesses such as influenza or fever. This help was especially important because poor people did not have easy access to professional medical care. In the states and cities on the East Coast, government agencies offered help in emergencies. However, in the huge territories in the north and the west, pioneers depended on neighbors for help during such disasters as fires, blizzards, storms, sickness, or violence.

When Fire Strikes

GET OUT! STAY OUT!

2   Now communities still depend on professional and volunteer workers in many agencies to help in all kinds of emergencies. For example, Red Cross volunteers help with over 67,000 emergencies every year. These include natural disasters, such as floods, hurricanes, and tornadoes, and manmade disasters, such as airplane crashes and car crashes.

C. Finish the sentences with words from the story.

1. _____ started the first volunteer fire department in Philadelphia, Pennsylvania.

2. In the early days, _____ often provided emergency medical help.

3. The _____ is a volunteer organization that provides help in a large number of emergency situations every year.

4. Natural disasters include _____, _____, and _____.

D. Read this excerpt of a song about the emergency that happened in New York City on September 11, 2001. Use your dictionary and talk with your class to learn words you don't know.

from "The Bravest"

The first plane hit the other tower
Right after I came in.
It left a gaping, firey hole
Where offices had been.
We stood and watched in horror
As we saw the first ones fall.
Then someone yelled "Get out! Get out!
They're trying to kill us all."

I grabbed the pictures from my desk
And joined the flight for life.
With every step I called the names
Of my children and my wife.
And then we heard them coming up
From several floors below.
A crowd of fire fighters,
With their heavy gear in tow.

CHORUS:
Now every time I try to sleep
I'm haunted by the sound,
Of firemen pounding up the stairs
While we were coming down
By Tom Paxton, 2001

Did You Know ?

Martha Ballard was a midwife who delivered 816 babies in Maine in the late 1700s and early 1800s. She wrote in her diary almost every day from 1785 to 1812—almost 10,000 entries. Because of Ballard's writing, people today know a lot about medical procedures, women's lives, and herbs and other remedies of the period.

3 Brainstorm ★

A. What kinds of emergencies happen in your community?

house and apartment fires

_____

_____

_____

B. List the people and organizations you can contact in an emergency.

the fire department

_____

_____

_____

4 Plan ★

Work in a small group to plan one of these projects.

★ Group 1: Find out how to contact all the emergency helpers in your community. This includes not only police, firefighters, EMTs, and hospitals, but also non-profit organizations and religious organizations.

★ Group 2: Look in community brochures, at the library, and on the Internet for things people can do to prepare for small or large emergencies. This can include finding out what building to go to if there is a bad storm and what radio station to listen to. Collect safety tips, such as regularly checking smoke detector batteries.

★ Group 3: Call up the local hospital or clinic, the local school, or the Red Cross for where and when you can take a class in first aid, CPR, or swimming safety. Some classes are free, but others may cost money.

★ Group 4: With your teacher or another school employee, investigate the entire building and grounds of the school for safety. Are all the lights working? Are there fire extinguishers and first aid kits in the building? Do the smoke detectors have good batteries? If there are any problems, make suggestions to make the school safe.

Where can you find information?

★ Look for pamphlets about getting help in your local community.

★ Look on the Internet.

★ Ask your doctor, someone at your health clinic, or a person at a local aid organization.

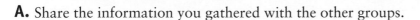

5 Community Experience: Emergency Help in Our Community

A. Share the information you gathered with the other groups.

B. Write down new information that is important to you.

EXAMPLE: The school first aid kit needs anti-bacterial cream.

_____

_____

_____

_____

_____

C. Decide how to share the emergency information your class gathered. Here are some suggestions.

★ Make a video about what you learned to show your families and friends. Some students can operate the camera, some can decide where to film; one student can act as the host, and one student can give information on camera.

★ Put together a book with information from all the groups so everyone has copies of the information.

★ Talk to other classes at the school. Make posters or other visual aids to help present the information.

★ Make a bulletin board display in your building or at the public library to share information with many people.

6 Reflect ★

Choose one of the topics below. Write about it in your journal, or talk about it with the class.

1. Describe an emergency that happened to you or someone you know.

2. The class learned information about finding help and helping out in an emergency. Do you think learning and then sharing information with others is a good way to learn English? Why or why not?

3. Some people think that you can avoid emergencies by preparing well. Other people think that good things and bad things just happen, and people have no control. What do you think?

7 Assess ★

What did you learn about being prepared and finding help in an emergency? What would you still like to learn? Fill in the chart with your own ideas and information.

I learned:	New words and phrases I want to remember:	I would like to learn more about:

Resources ★ ★ ★ ★ ★ ★ ★ ★ ★ ★ ★ ★ ★ ★ ★ ★

★ **Being prepared in an emergency**
Look in the 613–616 section of the public library. A book you might find is

> *The Survival Guide: What to do in a Biological, Chemical, or Nuclear Emergency* by Angelo Acquista. (2003). New York: Random House (adult level)

★ **Department of Homeland Security**
Information about this new federal department is available on the Internet at *www.dhs.gov/dhspublic/index.jsp* or by writing the U.S. Department of Homeland Security, Washington, D.C. 20528.

★ **Martha Ballard**
Martha Ballard's diary and other information are available on the Internet at *www.dohistory.org/diary/index.html*. For information about the video *A Midwife's Tale*, call PBS video at 1-800-344-3337.

LEARNING FOCUS

Content:

★ Types of health care and health insurance programs in the United States

Reading Skills:

★ Using a dictionary or glossary to learn new words

★ Taking notes

Civics Activities:

★ Identifying medical problems

★ Finding and sharing information about medical problems

Accessing Health Care

1 Think Ahead

Discuss these questions with a partner or small group.

★ Where are the people in these pictures?

★ What is happening in each picture?

★ What experiences have you had getting health care here or in your country?

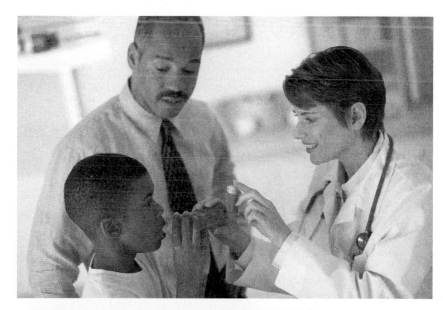

A. Read or listen to the passage. Circle the words you want to remember.

B. Use a dictionary or the glossary on pages 91–94 to learn about new words. Write new words and their definitions in your vocabulary notebook.

Health Care in the United States

Many English words have more than one meaning. For example, one meaning of *reservation* is an area of land owned by a Native American group. *To make a reservation* means to call in advance to get a table at a restaurant, a hotel room, or a seat on an airplane. *To have reservations about someone or something* means to have unanswered questions or concerns about someone or something.

1 There are many different types of health care services available in the United States. These services include isolated clinics on Native American reservations as well as gigantic university medical centers in big cities. Patients can access computer-assisted health care, visit a community health center, or find traditional folk medicine (such as special herbs) all in the same town.

Health Insurance Card
1234 Main Street • Anywhere, USA • 1800-555-1234

Group Number 0123 4567
Patient Name Jane Smith
Primary Care Physician Dr. John Doe, M.D.

2 There are almost 6,000 hospitals throughout the United States and approximately one doctor for every 345 people.* However, Americans do not all have the same access to medical care. For example, in Los Angeles County, California, with a population of over 9 million, there are 22,877 doctors. However, in rural Loving County, Texas, with a population of 67, there are no doctors.*

3 People come from around the world to get specialized medical help in American hospitals. Because of the high cost of medical care and because 14% of the people in the United States do not have health insurance, not everyone is able to receive good medical care when they need it. Medicaid and Medicare are government programs that help some Americans who are poor or elderly, who have disabilities, or who have other special problems. A new program called the State Children's Health Insurance Program now provides health care for children whose parents cannot afford it.

* U.S. Census 2000

C. Write one piece of information about each idea from the reading passage in the chart below.

Folk medicine	*Special herbs are a kind of folk medicine.*
Health insurance	
Medicaid and Medicare	
State Children's Health Insurance Program	

D. Answer these questions about yourself or someone you know.

EXAMPLE: Where did you go for medical care in your native country?
I went to the clinic in my town.

1. Where did you go for medical care in your native country?

_____

2. How can someone find a good doctor where you live now?

_____

3. Do you know a good way to pay for medical care?

_____

4. Where can a person find help for emotional and mental problems?

_____

E. Now talk with some of your classmates. Use a conversation starter.

EXAMPLES: Tell me about medical care in your native country.
Can you tell me how to find a good doctor in this area?

Did You Know?

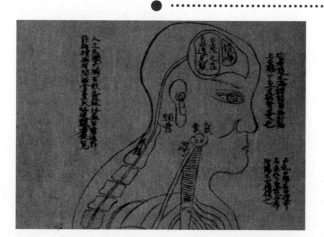

Acupuncture—inserting very thin narrow metal points in specific places in the body to regulate and gain spiritual, emotional, mental, and physical balance—has been used for health care in China for over 2,000 years. In the last 30 years, acupuncture has become increasingly popular in the United States. According to a 1998 study from Harvard University, Americans make about 5 million visits to acupuncturists each year.

3 Brainstorm ⭐

A. What do people in your community need to know about health care?

where to get immunizations

_____

_____

_____

B. List some of the problems people have with health care in the U.S.

not understanding the doctor

_____

_____

_____

4 Plan ⭐

Where can you find information?

★ Look in the government information pages of your local phone book for your public health department.

★ Look in the front of your phone book for hospital and health care listings.

★ Look in the yellow pages of your phone book under "Physicians."

★ Look on the Internet.

★ Ask your teacher or a friend for places to get more information about health care in your community.

Plan this project by yourself, with a partner, or with a small group of classmates. Follow these steps:

1. Identify a medical problem you would like to find out about. Describe the type of information you need.

   EXAMPLE: My mother thinks she has cancer. I would like to find a good doctor for her.

2. Make a list of questions you would like to ask about the problem.

   EXAMPLE: Where can I find a good cancer specialist?

3. Make a list of ways to contact people who know about this problem.

   EXAMPLE: Call the local health clinic for the name of a good doctor.

5 Community Experience: Health Care in Our Community

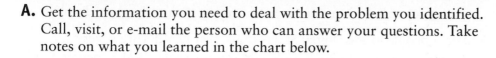

A. Get the information you need to deal with the problem you identified. Call, visit, or e-mail the person who can answer your questions. Take notes on what you learned in the chart below.

Problem	Person Contacted	Information

B. Share the information you learned with the class. Some medical information is personal, so you may not want to share it. Make a class list of the shared information. Type the information into the computer and make copies for everyone.

EXAMPLE:

Health Care in Our Community

★ For general health care information and referrals, call ___ .

★ To get advice about a medical problem on the Internet, go to ___ .

★ To find out about low cost dental care, call ___ .

★ To find out about health insurance, ask ___ .

★ To get help for a problem related to alcohol, call ___ .

★ To get help with translation, get in touch with ___ .

---

6 Reflect

A. Was your project successful? Circle your answers.

★ I **found/did not find** the information I needed.

★ The person I spoke to was **helpful/unhelpful.**

★ It was **easy/difficult** to communicate about health care in English.

★ I **will/will not** get more information about health care.

B. Choose one of the topics below. Write about it in your journal or talk about it with the class.

1. What did you think about working on a personal health project? Did your project help you in your life or to learn more English? Explain.

2. Some people in the United States think that health care is very expensive, especially for people without insurance. Other people think that the doctors here are great. What do you think?

3. Some people think that information about sex should be taught in schools. Other people think that only parents or religious people should discuss sex with children. What do you think?

7 Assess

What did you learn about health care in the United States? What would you still like to learn? Fill in the chart with your own ideas and information.

I learned:	New words and phrases I want to remember:	I would like to learn more about:

Resources ★ ★ ★ ★ ★ ★ ★ ★ ★ ★ ★ ★ ★ ★

★ **Acupuncture**
Go to the Website for the National Center for Complementary and Alternative Medicine at *www.nccam.nih.gov/health/acupuncture/index.htm*.

★ **Diseases**
Look in the 616 section of the public library. A book you might find is

> *Communicable Diseases* by Thomas H. Metos. (1987).
> New York: F. Watts. (elementary and secondary school
> level)

★ **Medicaid and Medicare**
The Website at *www.cms.hhs.gov/* gives official information about these programs, but you may need someone who knows a lot of English to help you understand it.

★ **State Children's Health Insurance Program**
Find information about your state's program on the Internet at *www.cms.hhs.gov/schip*. This information should also be available at your local health department, doctor's office, and public library.

CHAPTER 9

LEARNING FOCUS

Content:

* The rights and responsibilities of workers in the United States

Reading Skills:

* Using a dictionary or glossary to learn new words

* Reading for specific information

Civics Activities:

* Planning a panel discussion about workers' rights and responsibilities

* Inviting employers and employees to speak to the class

* Recording the panel discussion and sharing it with another class

Workers' Rights and Responsibilities

1 Think Ahead

Discuss these questions with a partner or a small group of your classmates.

* When and where do you think these pictures were taken?
* What are working conditions like in your native country?
* What more do you want to know about working conditions in the United States?

A. Read or listen to the passage. Circle the words you want to remember.

B. Read paragraph 1 or paragraph 2 again.

C. Use a dictionary or the glossary on pages 91–94 to learn about new words. Write new words and their definitions in your vocabulary notebook.

Dashes (—) are sometimes used to add extra information about a noun. The phrase *mostly single men* tells more about the Chinese immigrants who worked on the West Coast.

See page 95 for more information on John L. Lewis, Eugene Debs, and Walter Reuther.

Working in the United States

1   From the 1600s to the 1870s, the majority of men, women, and children in the United States lived and worked on farms or in small towns. Some people worked on family farms, and others worked on large plantations or ranches. Between 1870 and 1900, about 12 million immigrants entered the United States. Many immigrants got jobs in textile factories in Eastern cities and towns like Lowell, Massachusetts. In the Midwest, immigrants from Germany and Scandinavia homesteaded land for farming or worked in mines or forests. On the West Coast, Chinese immigrants—mostly single men—prospected for gold, helped build the railroads, and worked in restaurants, laundries, or on farms.

2   Working conditions were often bad. Women, men, and children all needed to work to make enough money to pay for food and rent. There were no benefits, such as health or life insurance, even if a person was hurt or died on the job. The wages for these difficult, boring, and dangerous jobs were often less than a dollar a day. Some workers—particularly miners, railroad workers, and later, auto workers—began to organize labor unions to fight for workers' rights. Union leaders such as John L. Lewis[2], Eugene V. Debs[3], and Walter Reuther[4] led strikes for better pay and working conditions. By the 1960s, millions of workers belonged to labor unions.

D. Finish the sentences with words from the paragraph you read.

PARAGRAPH 1

1. Before the twentieth century, some Americans worked on large
_____ or _____, but most worked on small
_____.

2. In the late 1800s, _____ immigrants came to live and
work in the United States.

3. On the West Coast, Chinese immigrants worked in many jobs, such as
_____, _____, or on
_____.

PARAGRAPH 2

1. Sometimes everyone in the family needed to work to make money for
_____ and _____.

2. Workers did not have health insurance or any other _____
to help them and their families even if they were hurt or died on
the job.

3. In the late 1800s and early 1900s, people organized _____
_____ to change bad working conditions.

E. Work with a partner who read the other paragraph. Ask and answer
questions so that you both understand the information in both
paragraphs.

EXAMPLES: What did you learn? What is the main idea of the paragraph?
What new vocabulary did you learn?

F. In a small group, talk about working conditions in your native
countries. Give specific examples from your own lives.

EXAMPLES: Do most workers get benefits in your native country? What
happens if someone is hurt on the job?

Did You Know ?

In the early 1900s, two-thirds of African-Americans
in the South were sharecroppers—farmers who
worked land they didn't own. These sharecroppers
worked hard but made very little money. One family
reported making only 15 cents profit in 1930! At the
same time, Northern cities needed more workers in
their factories. So, rural Southern African-Americans
as well as many others migrated to big industrial
cities like Chicago, Cleveland, Pittsburgh, Detroit, and
New York.

3 Brainstorm ★

A. Make a list of the rights and benefits workers need today.

sick days

B. What responsibilities do workers have on the job? List several examples.

get to work on time

4 Plan ★

A. Work in a small group to plan a panel discussion about workers' rights and responsibilities.

★ Group 1: Talk with the teacher about a specific topic for the discussion and about who to invite to be on the panel. For example, you could invite a local employer, a person from a local labor union or workers' rights group, and a worker (this can be a classmate). Decide on a good date and time, then call or write invitations.

★ Group 2: Write a list of questions to ask people on the panel about workers' rights, such as: *What happens if a worker is hurt on the job, but he or she doesn't have health insurance?*

★ Group 3: Write a list of questions about workers' responsibilities on the job, for example, *How do employers know a person is a good worker? What should a worker say if he or she needs to take time off work?*

★ Group 4: Make a plan for setting up the classroom and welcoming the guests. If you plan to record the discussion, arrange for audio or video equipment and appoint one or two classmates to be in charge of operating it.

B. Share your plans with the whole class. Listen to the other groups' plans and give advice.

C. Decide who will be the master of ceremonies (MC) for the discussion. The MC will introduce each panel member, supervise the question period, and keep time.

Where can you find information?

★ Talk to the teacher.

★ Talk to your employer.

★ Look on the Internet.

★ Check the government section of the telephone book.

In a panel discussion, each panel member usually has a few minutes to speak to the audience about the topic. Then the MC invites the audience to ask questions.

5 Community Experience: Exploring Employment Issues

A. Hold the panel discussion you planned. MC, set-up team, and questioners, do your jobs!

B. Take notes on the panel discussion in the chart below.

Speakers	Ideas/Information
Name: Organization:	1. _____ 2. _____ 3. _____
Name: Organization:	1. _____ 2. _____ 3. _____
Name: Organization:	1. _____ 2. _____ 3. _____

C. Look at your chart. What are the two most important things you learned from the panel?

_____

_____

D. Show the video or play the audiotape for another class. Invite the class to ask you questions about the panelists' ideas.

6 Reflect

Choose one of the topics below. Write about it in your journal, or talk about it with the class.

1. Who did your team invite for the panel discussion? What did you learn? Which speaker did you agree with the most? The least?

2. Do you think a panel discussion is a good idea? Why or why not? Were there any problems? What would you do differently next time?

3. Some people say the United States doesn't need labor unions anymore because the working conditions are good. Others say this country needs labor unions to protect the rights of all workers. What do you think?

7 Assess

What did you learn about working in the United States? What would you still like to learn? Fill in the chart with your own ideas and information.

I learned:	New words and phrases I want to remember:	I would like to learn more about:

Resources ★ ★ ★ ★ ★ ★ ★ ★ ★ ★ ★ ★ ★ ★ ★ ★

★ **Labor unions—history and people**
Look for information about the history of labor unions in the 973.8 or biography sections of the public library. A book you might find is

> *Bread—and Roses: The Struggle of American Labor 1865–1915* by Milton Meltzer. (2001). New York: Replica Books (elementary and secondary school level)

★ **Government regulations**
Contact OSHA (Occupational Safety and Health Administration, U.S. Department of Labor) at 1-800-321-6742 to report accidents, unsafe working conditions, or safety and health violations. For more information, go online to ***www.osha.gov***.

★ **Workers' compensation**
To read the rules about financial help for people who get hurt on the job, go to ***www.google.com***. In the search box, type *workers' compensation* and your state. For example:

workers' compensation California   Search

LEARNING FOCUS

Content:

* Places to live in the United States

Reading Skills:

* Using a dictionary or glossary to learn new words

* Reading for specific information

Civics Activities:

* Identifying housing in the community

* Finding out about rules for landlords and tenants

* Learning about the Fair Housing Act of 1968

* Finding out about financial assistance for housing

CHAPTER 10

Finding Good Places to Live

1 Think Ahead

Discuss these questions with a partner or small group.

* Which of the places in these pictures would you like to live in? Why?

* What do you know about finding good places to live in your community?

* What more do you want to know about housing in your community?

A. Read or listen to the reading passage. Circle the words you want to remember.

B. Use a dictionary or the glossary on pages 91–94 to learn about new words. Write new words and their definitions in your notebook.

Homes in the United States

> It is important to use respectful ways to talk about different ethnic and cultural groups. For example, the terms *Native American* and *African-American* are very respectful.

1   Most early European immigrants did not own a house or land in their native countries. For example, in England, Ireland, and Scotland, most people lived in small cottages on land owned by a few rich people. When the settlers came to North America from the 1600s to the 1800s, many people built cabins and developed their own small farms. This was a dream come true for the settlers, but they were building homes and farms on land that had been inhabited by Native Americans for many thousands of years. Wars about who owned the land continued until the early 1900s, and legal arguments still continue today.

2   According to the 2000 United States Census, 68% of households own their townhouses, houses, mobile homes, or condominiums.* Many families rent houses, apartments, or rooms. Finding good housing has been a challenge for many people because of discrimination and poverty. The Fair Housing Act, passed by Congress in 1968, made it illegal for owners to discriminate against renters or buyers. Although it is difficult to know for sure, one study reports that about 3.5 million people are homeless in any given year.** Many social, religious, and political groups try to make good housing available to everyone.

EQUAL HOUSING OPPORTUNITY

It is illegal to discriminate against any person because of race, color, religion, sex, or national origin.

* U.S. Census 2000
** National Coalition for the Homeless 2003

C. Finish the sentences with words from the reading.

1. From the 1600s to the 1800s, _____ and
_____ fought over land.

2. In the United States, most people _____ the places they
live in.

3. The Fair Housing Act made it _____ to refuse to rent
an apartment to people because of their race or national origin.

4. People who do not own their homes might live in _____,
_____, or _____.

5. Although most Americans can afford to live in houses or apartments,
there are over three million _____ people.

D. Work in a small group. Write a list of the types of housing in your
community. List the pros (advantages) and cons (disadvantages) of
each type.

Kinds of housing	Pros	Cons
condominiums	Management fixes problems outside.	association fees every month

Did You Know ?

Almost a thousand years before the Europeans came, the Anasazi people lived on high plateaus (or mesas) in homes carved out of cliffs, such as these at Mesa Verde National Park in southwestern Colorado. Some of the settlements were small, but Cliff Palace at Mesa Verde had over 200 rooms, including 23 communal or ceremonial rooms called *kivas*. The cliff dwellings also had storage areas and open areas for cooking.

3 Brainstorm

A. Make a list of things people need to know about housing in the United States.

tenants' rights

_____

_____

_____

B. Where can people get help with housing in your area? List the places you know.

community organization

_____

_____

_____

4 Plan

A. Work in small groups to plan one of these projects.

★ Group 1: Call or visit your local housing office and find out local rules for landlords and tenants. Ask if the office has these rules written in a brochure. Rules for tenants might be about paying rent and how many people can be in one apartment. Rules for landlords might be about not discriminating against individual people or groups.

★ Group 2: Call or visit a tenants' rights or home owners' group in your community. Make a list of questions to ask and collect information to share with the class.

★ Group 3: Find out more about the Fair Housing Act of 1968, a federal law that makes discrimination in housing illegal. With your teacher's help, take notes on the important parts of the law to share with the class.

★ Group 4: Find out how people without much money can get help with rent and paying for heat and electricity. Take notes to share with the class.

Where can you find information?

★ Call the library.

★ Look on the Internet.

★ Call or go to local government offices.

★ Ask your teacher, friends, or neighbors.

B. Answer the questions below about your group's plans.

1. Who will you contact for information?

   _____

2. What do you want to find out?

   _____

3. What questions will you ask?

   _____

   _____

   _____

5 Community Experience: Finding Out About Housing

A. Fill in answers to the questions about your call or visit.

Where did you call or visit?	
When did you call or visit?	
Who did you talk to?	
What did you learn about housing in your community?	

B. Look over your notes. Share the most important information you learned with the class. Then decide how your group can share the information with others in the community. For example, you could make a brochure to pass out at community meetings or at the library.

6 Reflect

Choose one of the topics below. Write about it in your journal, or talk about it with the class.

1. If you had all the money you needed, what kind of house would you like to live in? Describe it in words or pictures.

2. Many apartments don't allow people to keep pets such as cats and dogs. Is that a fair rule? Why or why not?

3. Discrimination on the basis of race, color, religion, sex, familial status, or national origin in renting a house or apartment has been illegal since 1968. Do you think everyone has equal opportunity for renting apartments or buying houses today? Support your opinion.

7 Assess

What did you learn about finding housing in the United States? What would you still like to learn? Fill in the chart with your own ideas and information.

I learned:	New words and phrases I want to remember:	I would like to learn more about:

Resources

★ **The Anasazi**

Look in the 97.3 section of the public library. A book you might find is

> *The Ancient Ones: The Anasazi of Mesa Verde* by
> Steven Otfinoski. (2002) Parsippany, NJ: Celebration
> Press/Pearson Learning Group (elementary school
> level)

★ **Fair Housing Act of 1968**

You can find information about this law at the library or on the U.S. Department of Justice Website at *www.usdoj.gov/kidspage/crt/housing.htm*.

★ **Tenants' rights groups**

Find contact information about renters' rights in each state online at *directory.tenantsunion.org/*.

Enjoying Local Parks and Recreation

Content:

★ Local parks and recreation services

Reading Skills:

★ Using a dictionary or glossary to learn new words

★ Scanning for specific details

★ Categorizing information

Civics Activities:

★ Planning a visit to a local recreation facility

★ Learning about the rules of a local recreation facility

★ Visiting a local recreation facility and obtaining information

1 | Think Ahead

Discuss these questions with a partner or small group.

★ What is happening in this picture?

★ What do you know about parks and recreation in your community?

★ What more do you want to know abouts parks and recreation near you?

A. Read or listen to the passage. Circle the words you want to remember.

B. Use a dictionary or the glossary on pages 91–94 to learn about new words. Write new words and their definitions in your vocabulary notebook.

Parks and Recreation

Information about where, when, or for what purpose something happens is often added to a sentence in a prepositional phrase. Here are some examples of prepositional phrases: *in New York City, in the last few years, for local residents.*

1   Most communities provide parks and recreation for local residents. However, opportunities for recreation differ from place to place. For example, Central Park in New York City has 843 acres and offers horseback riding, fishing, boating, a zoo, and Shakespeare plays. Even in the little town of Alpine, Texas, there are sports fields, a track, and a park for residents to use. Many communities support swimming programs and sports teams for children and adults. Some communities offer other leisure activities such as painting, crafts, cooking classes, and folk dancing.

2   Communities also organize special events. For example, the town of Lowell, Massachusetts, offers a free folk festival one weekend every summer. Community members from many ethnic groups perform music and dance, demonstrate arts and crafts, and sell homemade food. In the last few years, profit from selling the food—about $45,000—was donated back to the community. In 2002, residents of Arlington County, Virginia, planted 368 trees throughout the county to commemorate the victims of the September 11, 2001, terrorist attack on the Pentagon. Many activities and special events are funded by taxes people pay to the community, state, and federal government. Social, religious, and charitable organizations also support recreational activities. Playing soccer or music, enjoying nature, creating art or good food, and celebrating traditions are all ways Americans share in and improve their communities.

State parks offer many recreational activities.

C. Scan the reading passage for specific details and put them in the correct column on a sheet of paper.

Places	Activities
Central Park, New York City	boating

D. Write answers to the questions about your community.

EXAMPLE: Is there a park in your community?
Yes, there is. / No, there isn't.

1. Is there a park in your community?

   _____

2. If yes, have you visited it? If no, where is the nearest park?

   _____

3. In your native country, what was your favorite leisure activity?

   _____

4. What is your favorite leisure activity now that you live in the United States?

   _____

E. Form a small group and ask the same questions. Report to the class.

Did You Know?

The Midnight Basketball League was started in 1986, in Glenarden, Maryland, by G. Van Standifer. As town manager, he saw that a lot of crime happened between 10:00 p.m. and 2:00 a.m. To give teenagers and young adults something fun, safe, and useful to do late at night, Standifer organized basketball teams. Businesses and local organizations liked the idea and helped support it. Since 1986, the idea has spread to about 60 towns around the United States, helping young people and reducing crime.

3 Brainstorm

A. List some reasons why people should go out to parks.

get exercise

B. Why don't some people use the public parks and other recreational facilities?

don't know how to get there

4 Plan

Where can you find information?

★ Look at your community's official Website.

★ Check the government section of the telephone book, usually under "Parks and Recreation."

★ Look at community brochures.

★ Ask a friend or your teacher for ideas.

A. Work in small groups to plan for going to a local park, zoo, community garden, or museum.

★ Group 1: Investigate what places and activities are in or near your community.

★ Group 2: Find out about transportation. Draw a map or get information about buses or trains that stop near the place.

★ Group 3: Find out about the rules of the park. When does it open and close? Do you have to sign up for a tennis court or baseball field? Are pets allowed? Can people drink alcohol in the park?

★ Group 4: Make a class plan. When will people go to the place? How many people will go in cars? How many will walk? How many will take the bus? How many will go with classmates, with family, with friends, or alone?

B. Share your group's plan with the class.

C. Plan to find out about other recreational activities in the community, such as aerobics or painting classes. Write questions about the place, time, and cost of each activity and decide who you will call to ask.

5 Community Experience: At the Park or Recreation Center

A. Work alone, with a partner, or in a small group to find the following places and things in the park or recreation center you visit. Check (√) each one you find.

___ bathrooms   ___ information desk

___ drinking fountains   ___ office

___ telephone   ___ computers

___ information sign   ___ public telephones

___ area map   ___ _____

B. Write answers to these questions.

1. What place did you visit?

   _____

2. Who did you go with?

   _____

3. What did you do?

   _____

4. What did you enjoy about your visit?

   _____

5. Were there any problems? If so, what?

   _____

C. Take notes on the answers to your questions. Make a poster or brochure about recreational activities in your community to share with the class.

6 Reflect

Choose one of the topics below. Write about it in your journal, or talk about it with the class.

1. What did you think about the visit to the park or other facility? Will you go again? Why or why not? If you go, will you go alone or take someone with you? Who will you take? Why?

2. How important are sports and recreation to a person's life? Explain.

3. Communities have many important services to provide to the local residents, such as schools, roads, parks, and health and employment services. What service do you think is most important? Why?

7 Assess

What did you learn about parks and recreation in your community? What would you still like to learn? Fill in the chart with your own ideas and information.

I learned:	New words and phrases I want to remember:	I would like to learn more about:

Resources

★ **Arts, crafts, sports, and recreation**
Look for art books in the 700 section, look for crafts in the 745 section, and look for sports in the 796 section of the public library. A book you might find is

> *Family Sports Adventures: Exciting Vacations for Parents and Kids to Share* by Megan Stine. (1991). Boston, MA: Little, Brown (secondary school level)

The library will also have information about local recreation opportunities for children, adults, and families.

★ **Lowell Folk Festival**
Call 978-970-5000 or write to Lowell National Historical Park, 67 Kirk Street, Lowell, MA 01852. You can also look on the Internet at *www.lowellfolkfestival.org*.

★ **Midnight Basketball League**
Go online to *www.richmondmbl.org*.

CHAPTER 12

LEARNING FOCUS

Content:

* Protection of the natural environment

Reading Skills:

* Using a dictionary or glossary to learn new words
* Identifying the main idea
* Identifying specific details

Civics Activities:

* Finding information to start a recycling center at school
* Planning a class or family garden
* Learning about natural habitats
* Researching a community environmental problem

Helping Out With the Environment

1 Think Ahead

Discuss these questions with a partner or small group.

* What is happening in these pictures?
* What do you know about environmental problems here or in your native country?
* What more do you want to know about the environment?

A. Read or listen to the passage. Circle the words you want to remember.

B. Use a dictionary or the glossary on pages 91–94 to learn about new words. Write new words and their definitions in your vocabulary notebook.

🎧

Protecting the Natural Environment

1   When European explorers came to the New World in the 1600s, there were already several million people living in what is now Canada and the United States. The original inhabitants of North America hunted, fished, gathered wild foods, and farmed, but they did not overuse the environments they lived in. Now, according to the U.S. Census Bureau, approximately 285 million people live in the United States. Four hundred years of farming, logging, mining, industry, and population growth have caused serious degradation to air, water, and land.

Native Americans have lived in all environments, from the Arctic to Tierra del Fuego in Argentina.

> The prefix *de-* in the word *degradation* means "down" as in "getting worse."

2   Since the first Earth Day in spring, 1970, many individuals and groups have worked at the local, state, national, and international levels to preserve and improve the natural environment. Government jurisdictions have passed laws that help prevent further damage. Nowadays, environmental issues—the growing population, global warming, air and water pollution, limited natural resources, and increasing health problems—continue to concern individuals and communities.

C. Listen for more information about the environment. Write down the speaker's main idea.

_____

D. Listen again and list the specific details you hear.

EXAMPLE: asthma, air pollution

_____

_____

_____

See page 90 for the audioscript for Activities 2C and 2D.

E. Talk with your group about environmental problems in the United States or in other parts of the world. Make a list of places and problems.

Country	Environmental Problem
Brazil	_cutting down big sections of the Amazon rain forest_

Did You Know ?

The Great Lakes are located between the United States and Canada. See the map on pages 88–89. The Great Lakes are the largest source of surface fresh water on earth. In the 1960s, many people worried that Lake Erie, the shallowest of the five Great Lakes, was dying from industrial pollution flowing into the lake. The Canadian and United States governments and thousands of individuals and environmental groups worked together to save the lake. Today, Lake Erie provides a home for fish, birds, and other species as well as recreation for millions of people.

3 Brainstorm ★

A. Make a list of environmental problems in your community.

fish not safe to eat

_____

_____

_____

B. How can people help solve these problems? Name several ways.

learn how to clean up the lake

_____

_____

_____

4 Plan ★

A. Work in small groups to plan one of these projects. After you discuss the project with your group, write answers to the questions and report to the class.

Group 1: Start a recycling center at your school. Find out who you need to talk to and what steps you need to take.

Group 2: Plan a class or family garden. Find out where you can plant it. How big will it be? What will you grow?

Group 3: Learn about natural habitats in or near your community. Plan a trip to one of them with your class, family, or friends.

Group 4: Do research about a community environmental problem. How long has the problem existed? What are the causes? Organize a project to find out how you can solve it.

Where can you find information?

★ Call up or go to the library.

★ Look on the Internet.

★ Write environmental groups and ask for brochures.

★ Ask your teacher, your neighbors, and your friends for more information on local projects.

B. Answer the questions below about your group's plans.

1. What steps will the group take?

   a. _____

   b. _____

   c. _____

2. Who will you contact for information? _____

3. What will you need to complete your project? (Make a list.)

   _____   _____

   _____   _____

5 Community Experience: Helping Out With Your Local Environment

A. Follow your plan and complete your group's project. Use the grid below to report.

How did you get information? Where did you get it?	What did you learn about the community?	How did you help the environment?

B. Share the information you learned with your class or school. Write a paragraph, make a poster, or give an oral presentation to the class.

6 Reflect

A. Write about the project your group worked on. Tell what you did and describe any problems you had. Explain what you learned or how your project helped the community.

B. Choose one of the topics below. Write about it in your journal, or talk about it with the class.

1. Do you think helping the environment should be the job of the government or of community volunteers or of both? Explain.

2. Do you think companies or people who pollute the air, water, or land should pay to clean it up? Why or why not?

3. Some people think that saving trees or animals is not as important as people being able to have jobs and homes. What do you think?

7 Assess

What did you learn about helping with the environment in your community? What would you still like to learn? Fill in the chart with your own ideas and information.

I learned:	New words and phrases I want to remember:	I would like to learn more about:

Resources

★ **The environment**
Look in the 363.7 section of the public library. Some books you might find are

Earth Day by Mir Tamim Ansary. (2002). Chicago: Heinemann Library (elementary school level)

Global Warming: Opposing Viewpoints edited by James Haley. (2002). San Diego, California: Greenhaven Press

★ **Protecting the environment**
Call the U.S. Environmental Protection Agency (EPA) at 1-202-260-2090. Before you call, have your questions ready. You can find the address for regional EPA centers on the Internet at ***www.epa.gov***.

13

Content:
* Life in a multicultural country

Reading Skills:
* Using a dictionary or glossary to learn new words
* Reading for specific information

Civics Activities:
* Finding out where languages of the world are spoken
* Getting information about future cultural activities in the community
* Sharing information about a local cultural event
* Hosting a class or school multicultural event

Living Together in a Multicultural Land

1 Think Ahead

Discuss these questions with a partner or small group.

* What is happening in this picture?
* Do different groups of people live together in your native country? How are they different from each other? What languages do they speak?
* What do you know about different cultural groups who live in your community here? What more do you want to know?

A. Read or listen to the reading passage. Circle the words you want to remember.

B. Use a dictionary or the glossary on pages 91–94 to learn about new words. Write new words and their definitions in your vocabulary notebook.

The United States: Out of Many—One

Use **past tense** verbs (*came, had*) to talk about completed past events. Use **present perfect** verbs (*have struggled*) to talk about events or conditions that are still true.

See page 95 for more information on the following languages: Quechua, Korean, Amharic, Tagalog, Hmong, Urdu, Vietnamese, Arabic, Spanish, and Mandarin.

1   When the European explorers came to North America in the 1500s there were already about 300 distinct cultural groups living on the continent. In the following century, settlers from England became the largest European immigrant group in the thirteen colonies. Many others came from France, Germany, the Netherlands, Spain, and other countries. West Africans were captured and brought to North America as slaves. Throughout U.S. history, some groups have had more civil rights than others. Other groups have struggled for equal rights and opportunities.

The Great Seal of the United States

2   Currently, immigrants come to the United States from all over the world. Native speakers of Quechua[5], Korean, Amharic[6], Tagalog[7], Hmong[8], Urdu[9], Vietnamese, Arabic[10], Spanish, Mandarin[11], and French may all have children in the same elementary school class. For example, children in the Montgomery County, Maryland, schools come from over 161 countries! Languages, customs, and religions vary, but many millions of immigrants and native-born people share the name "American."

C. Finish the sentences with words from the reading.

1. In the 1500s, about _____ cultural groups were living in North America.

2. The largest European immigrant group in the thirteen colonies was the _____ settlers.

3. Today, people from all over the _____ come to live in the United States.

4. Some groups have had to struggle for _____ rights and opportunities.

D. Talk together in a small group. Find where in the world the languages from the story come from. Use the notes in Appendix F on page 95 to help you.

Quechua	*Bolivia, Peru*
Korean	
Amharic	
Tagalog	
Hmong	
Urdu	
Vietnamese	
Arabic	
Spanish	
Mandarin	
French	

Did You Know ?

In the United States, Christianity is the largest religion with an estimated 160 million adult followers. Judaism has an estimated 3 million adult followers, while Islam and Buddhism each have an estimated 1 million adult followers. Hinduism, Sikhism, Baha'i and Native American religions have many followers as well. In this photo, representatives of several religions pray in Yankee Stadium at the memorial service for victims of the tragedy of September 11, 2001.

3 Brainstorm

A. Make a list of things that help keep immigrant cultures strong.

music

_____

_____

_____

B. Think of reasons why some immigrants don't stay connected to their home cultures.

don't have time

_____

_____

_____

4 Plan

Where can you find information?

★ Call the library.

★ Look on the Internet.

★ Check your local newspaper.

★ Check local grocery stores for bulletin board announcements.

A. Work in small groups to plan for attending a local cultural event, fair, concert, or festival.

★ Group 1: Get information about upcoming cultural events in your community. Find out when and where the event is happening.

★ Group 2: Decide what additional information you need (for example, directions, cost, what to wear). Decide what questions you want to ask. Call the group or person who is organizing the event and get the information.

★ Group 3: Find out about transportation to the event.

★ Group 4: Make a class plan. When and where will the class meet? How many people will walk? How many will take the bus?

B. Plan for your own class or school multicultural show or exhibit and invite the community to come.

★ Group 1: Find out who in your class would like to make an exhibit to share history, clothes, crafts, music, poetry or photographs. Make a list of what each person will do.

★ Group 2: Plan to take photographs or videotape the event. Who will bring a camera? What will you take pictures of?

★ Group 3: Talk to your teacher about a good day and time. Decide who you would like to invite to the exhibit. Make posters and/or write invitations to the people you hope will come.

★ Group 4: Decide on a good name for your show or exhibit. Write out a program to give to people when they arrive.

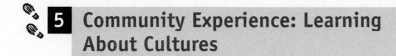

5 Community Experience: Learning About Cultures

A. Enjoy your visit to the local cultural event. Then fill in answers to the questions in the chart below.

Where did you go?	
When did you go?	
Who did you talk to?	
What did you see, hear, do, or listen to?	
What did you like most?	
What did you like least?	

B. Follow your plan for hosting a show or exhibit. Take photographs and talk to the people who come. Take notes on their comments. Share the experience by presenting an exhibit of photos, showing the video, or making a book of pictures and comments for the class to keep.

6 Reflect

Choose one of the topics below. Write about it in your journal, or talk about it with the class.

1. Do you think it is important to keep parts of your native culture and language here in the United States? If yes, how? If no, why not?

2. In 1962, the U.S. Supreme Court declared that children and teachers may not participate in organized spoken prayers in class. Some people think this is a good law; some people do not. What do you think?

3. In his famous 1963 speech called "I Have a Dream," Martin Luther King, Jr., said that people should be judged, "not by the color of their skin, but by the content of their character." What does this statement mean to you?

7 Assess

What did you learn about living in a multicultural land? What would you still like to learn? Fill in the chart with your own ideas and information.

I learned:	New words and phrases I want to remember:	I would like to learn more about:

Resources ★

★ **E Pluribus Unum and The Great Seal of the United States**
Go to *bensguide.gpo.gov/3-5/symbols/seal.html*.

★ **Immigration, slavery and civil rights, women in America**
Search the American Memory Internet site at *memory.loc.gov/ammem/ndlpedu/features/index.html*.

★ **Native Americans before the Europeans came**
Look in the 970.1–973 section of the public library. Two books you might find are

North American Indian Life by John D. Clare. (2000).
Hauppague, NY: Barron's Educational Series
(elementary school level)

In the Hand of the Great Spirit: The 20,000-year History of American Indians by Jake Page. (2003).
New York: Free Press. (adult level)

Making a Difference in the Community

1 Think Ahead

Discuss these questions with a partner or small group.

★ What is happening in these pictures?
★ Who do you think the people are?
★ What more do you want to know about these people?

A. Read or listen to the passage. Circle the words you want to remember.

B. Use a dictionary or the glossary on pages 91–94 to learn about new words. Write new words and their definitions in your vocabulary notebook.

Volunteering in the Community

The word *volunteer* comes from the Latin verb *velle* (to be willing) and a related noun, *voluntas* (will or desire). When you *volunteer,* you help other people but you don't get paid.

See page 95 for more information on the Lions, Girl Scouts, and Boy Scouts.

1   Volunteering is a tradition in communities throughout the United States. In the pioneer days, communities were able to survive in harsh conditions because neighbors helped each other. Now, many people continue to offer help to those who are poor, elderly, ill, or have special needs. Some people volunteer through their religious organizations, schools, and community groups, such as Lions[12], Girl Scouts[13], Boy Scouts[14], and local civic associations. Some volunteers help by cooking and serving food to homeless people. Others help teach children to read or provide assistance to people who need help with their income tax forms.

2   For those who do not have time to volunteer on a regular basis, there are occasional events such as walks, races, or bake sales to raise money for people in need. There are also opportunities to volunteer to help during natural disasters such as floods, hurricanes, and earthquakes. For example, owners of four-wheel-drive vehicles often volunteer to drive doctors and nurses to hospitals during snowstorms. Volunteers have also rushed to the aid of victims of other tragedies. After the September 11, 2001, terrorist attacks in New York and Washington, D. C., thousands of people volunteered to help. In all of these ways, community members—children, adults, elders, citizens, and newcomers—help each other build and maintain strong and friendly places to live.

C. Listen for more information about volunteering. Write the speaker's main idea below.

_____

D. Listen again and list the specific details you hear.

AIDS Clinic _____

_____

_____

See page 90
for the
audioscript
for Activities
2C and 2D.

E. Answer the questions below about yourself.

EXAMPLE: In what ways do people help the community in your native country?
In my village, many people worked together to build a new clinic.

1. In what ways do people help the community in your native country?

_____

_____

2. Do you think it is important to volunteer in the community? Why or why not?

_____

_____

F. Now talk with some of your classmates about volunteering in their native countries. Make a list of examples below.

_____

_____

Did You Know ?

In the United States, volunteers help find people who are lost or in danger. Many volunteers help search and rescue operations in the West because there are thousands of miles of wilderness in the mountains, deserts, and forests. Sometimes hikers get lost, skiers get caught in avalanches, or airplanes and helicopters crash. The volunteers receive training and help out when needed.

3 Brainstorm

A. Make a list of people who need help in your community.

homeless people

_____

_____

_____

B. List some reasons why it may be difficult for some people to volunteer.

very busy

_____

_____

_____

4 Plan

Where can you find information?

★ Look for the volunteer office of your local government in the telephone book.

★ Call the reference librarian and ask for information about local volunteer groups and upcoming events.

★ Look on your community's Website.

★ Ask your friends and neighbors.

A. Work in small groups to find out about opportunities for volunteering in your community. Here is one way to organize the groups.

Group 1: Find out how to contact the volunteer office of your local government. Ask for a brochure or information about where and how to volunteer, or ask someone to come talk to the class.

Group 2: Plan to call up the local hospital or clinic. Make a list of questions about volunteer opportunities. You may want to find out if there is a need for people to help patients who don't speak English well.

Group 3: Plan to get information about volunteering at the local elementary school. Someone from your group could call or go to the school and ask for a list of volunteer jobs, times, and skills needed.

Group 4: Get information about volunteering in your community from your own civic or social group, religious group, or neighborhood association.

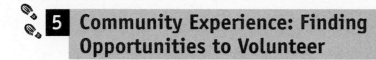
A. Call or visit the organization you chose. Bring back as much information as you can, or take notes on the answers to your questions.

B. Organize the information you collected and your notes in the chart below.

Place	Ways to Volunteer	Benefits	Other Information

C. Share your information with the class.

D. Work alone to circle or write the appropriate information on the following form.

Volunteer Association

NAME _____

ADDRESS _____

TELEPHONE _____ Best time to call _____

I am able to volunteer now.　　YES　　NO　　MAYBE

I want to volunteer because _____

I want to help by _____

(Example: *answering phone calls in my language*)

My special skills are _____

I want to help on _____ (day/s) at _____ (time)

I am able to help:　　one time　　every week　　when there is an emergency

---

E. If you wish, contact the organization of your choice, and make arrangements to begin working as a volunteer.

6 Reflect

Choose one of the topics below. Write about it in your journal, or talk about it with the class.

1. Many people donate their time and hard work to help others. Some people just give money to help. Do you think giving money is as helpful as volunteering? Why or why not?

2. Some people think that volunteering is so important that high schools should require every student to volunteer in the community. Do you think that is a good idea? Explain.

3. Sometimes people or groups send letters asking for money. Some of these groups are responsible charities, but some are trying to steal your money. What are some ways you can find out if the group is legitimate?

7 Assess

What did you learn about volunteering in your community? What would you still like to learn? Fill in the chart with your own ideas and information.

I learned:	New words and phrases I want to remember:	I would like to learn more about:

Resources ★ ★ ★ ★ ★ ★ ★ ★ ★ ★ ★ ★ ★ ★ ★ ★

★ **Volunteering**
Look in the 361.37 section of the public library. Two books you might find are

> *Making a Difference: Your Guide to Volunteering and Community Service* by Arthur I. Blaustein. (2002). Berkeley, CA: Heyday Books (adult level)

> *United We Stand* by Nancy Louis (2002). Edina, MN: Abdo Publishing Co. (secondary school level)

The public library will also have information about where and how you can volunteer in your own community.

★ **Search and rescue groups**
Look on the Internet at ***www.google.com***. Type *search and rescue* and the name of your state.
For example:

search and rescue Minnesota	Search

Appendix A

Bill of Rights

Amendment I

Congress shall make no law respecting an establishment of religion, or prohibiting the free exercise thereof; or abridging the freedom of speech, or of the press; or the right of the people peaceably to assemble, and to petition the Government for a redress of grievances.

Amendment II

A well regulated Militia, being necessary to the security of a free State, the right of the people to keep and bear Arms, shall not be infringed.

Amendment III

No Soldier shall, in time of peace be quartered in any house, without the consent of the Owner, nor in time of war, but in a manner to be prescribed by law.

Amendment IV

The right of the people to be secure in their persons, houses, papers, and effects, against unreasonable searches and seizures, shall not be violated, and no Warrants shall issue, but upon probable cause, supported by Oath or affirmation, and particularly describing the place to be searched, and the persons or things to be seized.

Amendment V

No person shall be held to answer for a capital, or otherwise infamous crime, unless on a presentment or indictment of a Grand Jury, except in cases arising in the land or naval forces, or in the Militia, when in actual service in time of War or public danger; nor shall any person be subject for the same offence to be twice put in jeopardy of life or limb; nor shall be compelled in any criminal case to be a witness against himself, nor be deprived of life, liberty, or property, without due process of law; nor shall private property be taken for public use, without just compensation.

Amendment VI

In all criminal prosecutions, the accused shall enjoy the right to a speedy and public trial, by an impartial jury of the State and district wherein the crime shall have been committed, which district shall have been previously ascertained by law, and to be informed of the nature and cause of the accusation; to be confronted with the witnesses against him; to have compulsory process for obtaining witnesses in his favor, and to have the Assistance of Counsel for his defence.

Amendment VII

In suits at common law, where the value in controversy shall exceed twenty dollars, the right of trial by jury shall be preserved, and no fact tried by a jury, shall be otherwise reexamined in any Court of the United States, than according to the rules of the common law.

Amendment VIII

Excessive bail shall not be required, nor excessive fines imposed, nor cruel and unusual punishments inflicted.

Amendment IX

The enumeration in the Constitution, of certain rights, shall not be construed to deny or disparage others retained by the people.

Amendment X

The powers not delegated to the United States by the Constitution, nor prohibited by it to the States, are reserved to the States respectively, or to the people.

Appendix B

Rights of All Immigrants

All people in the U.S. have certain rights. It does not matter if you are a U.S. citizen, a permanent resident, or undocumented. What are these rights?

All Rights in National and State Labor Law This includes the right for most workers to receive at least the minimum wage. Most services in government-funded clinics are free or low cost for poor people.

Emergency Any hospital emergency room, critical care unit, or intensive care unit cannot deny treatment for a very serious medical problem.

Immunizations Free vaccinations are available for diseases such as tuberculosis, tetanus, and polio.

Most Rights Guaranteed under the Constitution and the Bill of Rights This includes the right to practice whatever religion you want and to gather together with other people peacefully to request changes in the government. If you are arrested for a crime, you have the right to remain silent, get a free lawyer, talk to a lawyer before you answer any questions, and have a lawyer with you while you answer any questions.

Nutrition Programs Poor people have the right to free school breakfast and lunch, soup kitchens, community food banks, and other nutrition programs for adults and families.

Public School Public elementary and high school education is available and required for all school-age children.

Short-term Shelter and Housing If there is space at a battered women's shelter or homeless shelter, you cannot be turned away because of your legal status. All immigrants can also receive housing during a natural disaster (hurricane, floods).

Testing and Treatment for Symptoms of Communicable Diseases Free or low-cost testing and some treatment is available for infectious diseases such as AIDS, syphilis, gonorrhea, measles, tuberculosis, leprosy, diphtheria, and scarlet fever.

Violence Prevention Programs Counseling, advocacy, support groups, and training on gangs, domestic violence, child abuse, and similar crises cannot be denied because of your immigration status.

Appendix C

CANADA

MINNESOTA

L. Superior

MICHIGAN

WISCONSIN
★ St. Paul

L. Michigan

L. Huron

Lansing ★

IOWA
Des Moines ★

Madison ★

ILLINOIS

INDIANA

OHIO
Columbus ★

Springfield ★

Indianapolis ★

Topeka ★

Jefferson
City ★

MISSOURI

Charleston ★
★ Frankfort

WV

KENTUCKY

Nashville ★

ARKANSAS

Little
Rock ★

Mississippi

TENNESSEE

ALABAMA

MISSISSIPPI

Atlanta ★

Jackson ★

GEORGIA

Montgomery ★

Baton Rouge ★
LOUISIANA

Tallahassee ★

FLORIDA

Gulf of Mexico

St. Lawrence R.

MAINE

★ Augusta

Montpelier ★ NH

Concord ★

VT

Boston ★

Albany ★

MA

NEW
YORK

Hartford ★

Providence ★

CT

RI

40°N

PENNSYLVANIA

Harrisburg ★

Trenton ★

NEW JERSEY

Dover ★

APPALACHIAN MOUNTAINS

MD

DELAWARE

Annapolis
Washington, D.C. ★

★ Richmond

VIRGINIA

Raleigh ★

NORTH
CAROLINA

Columbia ★

SOUTH
CAROLINA

ATLANTIC
OCEAN

30°N

BAHAMAS

CUBA

| 0 | 300 mi |
| 0 | 300 km |

N
W   E
S

Appendix D

Listening Script

Chapter 12, Activities 2C and 2D.

My name is Kara Kukovich. I'm just starting college in the fall. I was born and lived all my life in Arlington, Virginia. Right now, I'm working with a community organization that works to help the local environment. I'm very concerned about the environment. Since I was in high school, I've helped check the water quality of the streams in Arlington. I can tell whether the water is clean by seeing what kinds of insects live in it. This is important because these streams go into the Potomac River and then into the Chesapeake Bay and the Atlantic Ocean.

I am also concerned about air pollution. All my life I've felt physically sick when I go into the city—that's Washington, DC. Washington has had an increase in dangerous air alerts the last couple of years. We call them "code red" days. Those days are hard on small children, older people, and people who have diseases like asthma. Some environmental groups around here have sued the federal government over air pollution.

The college I will go to this fall has a lot of classes about the environment, so that will be good for me.

Chapter 14, Activities 2C and 2D.

My name is Genevieve Darghouth. I am originally from Grenoble, France, but I've lived in Arlington, Virginia for more than 20 years. I am a volunteer worker at the Whitman-Walker Clinic in Washington, DC. This clinic helps people who have HIV or AIDS. I help deliver psychotherapy to French-speaking Africans at the clinic and help them solve many different kinds of problems related to health care and social services. Sometimes, I use my French and English skills to help interpret and advocate for my clients.

I think there are three reasons I volunteer. First, many years ago, I had cancer. The hospital and the doctors here gave me very good care and I am healthy now. So, I feel I need to give back to the community to say thanks for that. Second, several years ago a good friend of mine died of AIDS in France, and I was not there to help him. Instead, I now help people in similar situations. Third, before I was a professional therapist, but I get much more emotional satisfaction helping people at the clinic than when I had the paid job.

Appendix E

Glossary

The numbers in parentheses are the chapters in which the terms appear.

agency	a part of government that does a specific job. For example, the Office of Safety and Health Administration (OSHA) helps protect workers. (7)
assembly	the meeting or coming together of a group to talk about business, politics, religion, and other things. (2)
bake sale	selling cakes, cookies, pies, and so on to make money to help a school, church, or sports team. (14)
benefit	non-money payment to workers, for example, health insurance, sick leave, and paid vacation. (9)
Bill of Rights	the first ten amendments to the U.S. Constitution; they were added in 1791. (6)
board	in some local governments, a group of people elected or appointed to govern. Many cities, towns, and counties have school boards. (5)
boycott	joining with others to refuse to buy things, do work, or use transportation to force a change, for example, the Montgomery, Alabama, bus boycott in 1955-56. (1)
charitable organization	an organization that raises money to help others, for example, Save the Children, the Red Cross, and the World Wildlife Fund. (11)
check out	to take books, cassettes, or videos from a library, using a library card, and agree to bring them back on time. (4)
citizen	a person, native born or legally accepted, who has all the rights of a country, for example, the right to vote. (5)

civic association	a group of people in a community who volunteer to work together to help their neighborhood. They might have community parties or take food to elderly people. (14)
colony	an area of land settled by people from another country and governed by the other country. (1)
commemorate	to remember someone or something important with a special event or monument. (11)
commonwealth	an area that belongs to a country but is independent in some ways, especially in local laws. Puerto Rico and the Northern Mariana Islands are U.S. commonwealths. (5)
community resources	useful places and services in a community, for example, libraries, swimming pools, schools, clinics, hospitals, and parks. (4)
computer-assisted health care	diagnosis and treatment of sick people with computerized or electronic equipment. (8)
county	a division of a state in the United States. Hawaii and Delaware each have 3 counties; Texas has 254 counties. (5)
court	the place where a judge decides what laws mean and how they should be applied. (6)
degradation	the condition of changing for the worse. Too much fishing and too many chemicals in the water have caused a degradation of the oceans. (12)
discriminate	to treat one group of people differently from the way you treat other people, especially to treat that group unfairly. (10)
dream come true	a strongly held wish that actually happens, like the happy ending in a children's story. (10)
Earth Day	a special day first celebrated on April 22, 1970, to help people learn how to help save the environment. (12)
ethnic group	a group of people who share the same culture and language. (11)
federal	the highest level of the U.S. government. The federal government is located in Washington, D.C. (5)
First Amendment	an addition to the Constitution that gives people the freedom to say and write what they want, to choose their own religion (or no religion), to get the news freely, to meet in groups, and to ask for changes in the government. (2)
folk medicine	traditional forms of medicine, such as treatment with herbs and acupuncture. (8)
global warming	process of the earth's atmosphere getting warmer over time. (12)
health insurance	a system to help people pay for medical treatment. A person pays money every month to an insurance company. When treatment is needed, the company will pay all or most of the medical bill. (8)

homeless	without a permanent home. Homeless people often stay on the street or in shelters. (10)
homestead	to settle on land given by the government in return for farming and living there. In the nineteenth century, much of the West was settled by homesteading. (9)
household	all the people living together in one house or apartment. (10)
income tax form	a document that reports how much money a worker must pay to the government. (4)
judge	a public official who decides the law and decides cases (trials) in a court. (6)
labor union	an organized group of workers who bargain with their employer for wages and benefits. Some workers are in unions, but many are not. (9)
life insurance	a system to help the family of a person who dies. A person pays money every month to an insurance company. When he or she dies, the family gets money from the company. (9)
Medicaid	federal government money for health care for poor people or people with disabilities. The rules are different from state to state. (8)
Medicare	national health insurance for people over 65 and some people with disabilities. (8)
migrant farm workers	farm workers who travel from place to place to plant, grow, and harvest vegetables and fruits. Many migrant farm workers come from Mexico, the Caribbean, and Central America. (1)
Native American	the first people to settle in North, Central, and South America. (1)
natural resources	air, land, water, animals, and plants that humans use. (12)
New World	name given to the Western Hemisphere (North, Central, and South America) by European explorers. (12)
Pentagon	the main office building of the United States military in Arlington, Virginia; it is named that because the building has five sides. (11)
permanent resident	an immigrant who is legally allowed to stay in the United States for the rest of his or her life. (5)
pioneer	a person who settles a new area. The first white people to move west in the eighteenth and nineteenth centuries are called pioneers. (3)
plantation	a large farm, especially in the southern United States, that grew only a few crops, such as cotton, tobacco, or sugar cane. Many enslaved people worked on plantations. (9)
press	originally, newspapers and magazines; now all types of media, such as television, radio, and the Internet. (2)

probable cause	a reasonable idea that an illegal activity is going on. Police can enter a person's house only if they believe something illegal is happening there. (6)
recycle	to remake and use something again to save materials, for example, glass, paper, and metal. (2)
religious freedom	part of the First Amendment to the U.S. Constitution. It says that religion cannot be part of the government. (1)
right	a power or privilege that belongs legally or morally to a person or people; the United States was founded on the idea that everyone has some basic rights. (2)
shelter	a place that provides food, a place to sleep, and sometimes counseling and health services. There are homeless shelters and shelters for abused women and children. (2)
slavery	a system that takes freedom away from people. The enslaved people have to work for others. Slavery was legal in parts of the United States until 1865. (1)
State Children's Health Insurance Program	a federal government program to give medical help to poor children. The rules are different from state to state. (8)
strike	organized workers stopping work to force an employer to provide higher wages or better benefits. (9)
territory	an area that belongs to a country but does not have all the rights of a state. Guam is a territory of the United States. (5)
textile factory	a factory where cloth or clothing is made. Steam and electricity powered many textile factories. (9)
township	a local government in parts of the United States, especially in the Northeast and Midwest. (5)
trauma injury	an injury caused by an accident or violence, for example, broken legs and arms, serious cuts, and gunshot wounds. (7)
Underground Railroad	a secret system of people and safe houses that helped slaves escape to the northern states and Canada. About 100,000 people used the Underground Railroad to gain their freedom. (1)
undocumented person	a person who does not have papers such as a birth certificate, work permit, green card, or visa that allows him or her to live and work in the United States. (5)
U.S. Constitution	a document that describes the type of government and laws of the United States. (2)

Appendix F

Notes

These names are referenced in the readings with the numbers given here.

1. **Benjamin Franklin** (1706–1790) was one of America's most famous and respected leaders. He was a printer, philosopher, scientist, and political and social leader.

2. **John L. Lewis** (1880–1969) was a union organizer for miners who helped organize workers in other industries and get benefits for them.

3. **Eugene V. Debs** (1855–1926) was an early labor organizer and politician. He was involved in railroad strikes in the 1890s.

4. **Walter Reuther** (1907–1970), the son of German immigrants, was a factory worker who became the president of a strong labor union.

5. **Quechua** (noun or adjective) is a language spoken by many Native Americans in Peru, Bolivia, and neighboring countries.

6. **Amharic** (noun or adjective) is a language spoken by people in Ethiopia and Eritrea.

7. **Tagalog** (noun) is the official language of the Republic of the Philippines.

8. **Hmong** (noun and adjective) is a language and an ethnic group of Southeast Asia; most of the Hmong in the United States came from Laos after the Vietnam War, which ended in 1975.

9. **Urdu** (noun or adjective) is the official language of Pakistan; it is also spoken in India.

10. **Arabic** (noun or adjective) is the language spoken by over 180,000,000 people throughout the world. It originated in the area now called Saudi Arabia.

11. **Mandarin** (noun or adjective) is one of the many languages of China; it is spoken by more people than any other language in the world.

12. **Lions** (noun) form one of many volunteer, charitable organizations that help people in their community. For example, Lions support children's sports teams and help blind people.

13. **Girl Scouts** is an organization for girls and young women for learning skills—from camping to computers—and moral values; it was started in 1912.

14. **Boy Scouts** is an organization for boys and young men for moral, physical, and educational development; it was started in 1910.

Index

A
acupuncture, 45
advertisements, 16
African-Americans, 3, 51, 56
    migration north, 51
aid, 38
AIDS, 38
airplane crash, 38
alcohol, 33
Alpine, Texas, 62
Amharic, 74, 75, 95
Anasazi people, 57, 60
anthropology, 9
Arabic, 74, 75, 95
Arlington County, Virginia, 62
assessment, 6, 12, 18, 24, 30, 36, 42, 48,
    54, 60, 66, 72, 78, 84
audio-visual department of library, 23

B
Baha'i, 75
Ballard, Martha, 39, 42
Bill of Rights, 32, 85–86
biography section of library,
    24, 54
Boston, Massachusetts, 14, 38
Boy Scouts, 80, 97
boycott, 2
"Bravest, The" (Paxton), 39
Buddhism, 75
bulletin boards, 41, 76
businesses, 11

C
car crash, 38
Carnegie, Andrew, 20
census, 26, 44, 56, 68
Central Park, 62
Chavez, Cesar, 2
children's room in library, 23
Chinese immigrants, 50
Christianity, 75
circulation desk, 23
civic participation, 1–6
civil rights, 36, 74
commonwealth, 26

community, 7–12. *See also* civic
    participation
condominiums, 56, 57
county government, 26
courthouse, 34–36
cultural events, 76
cultural groups, 73–78

D
dashes (punctuation), 50
Debs, Eugene V., 50, 95
dictionary. *See* glossary
disasters, 38, 39
discrimination, 56, 60
doctors, 44

E
E Pluribus Unum, 78
Earth Day, 68
education, 13–18
Eighteenth Amendment, 33
emergencies, 37–42
emergency aid workers, 38, 40. *See also*
    volunteers
English immigrants, 2, 74
environment, 67–72
Environmental Protection Agency, 72
ethnic terms, 56
European immigrants, 2, 56, 74

F
facts, 5
Fair Housing Act, 56–58, 60
farming, 14, 50, 56
    sharecroppers, 51
federal government, 26
fire departments, 38
floods, 38
folk medicine, 44, 45
Franklin, Benjamin, 38, 95
freedom of speech, 24
French, 74, 75

G
gardens, 70
German immigrants, 50, 74
Girl Scouts, 80, 95

glossary, 2, 8, 14, 20, 26, 32, 38, 44, 50,
    56, 62, 68, 74, 80, 91–94
government. *See also* local government
    levels of, 26
    regulations, 54
    Websites, 30, 48, 54, 60, 72, 78
Great Lakes, 69
Greensboro, North Carolina, 3
guest speakers, 16, 17, 35, 52

H
Harvard College, 14
health care, 43–48
health insurance, 44, 45
Hinduism, 75
Hmong, 74, 75, 95
home ownership, 56
home schools, 14
homelessness, 56
hospitals, 44
housing, 55–60
hurricanes, 38

I
immigrants, 30, 36, 50, 56, 73–78
    rights of, 36, 87
information. *See also* resources; Websites,
    5, 17, 22, 29, 34, 41, 46, 47, 52, 58–59,
    64, 70, 71, 76, 82
    prepositional phrases and, 62
Internet. *See* Websites
Islam, 75

J
Jamestown colony, 2
"Jim Crow" laws, 3
job benefits, 50
journal writing, 6, 12, 18, 24, 30, 36, 42,
    48, 54, 60, 66, 72, 78, 84
Judaism, 75
jurisdiction, 26
justice, 32

K
King, Martin Luther, Jr., 78
kivas, 57
Korean, 74, 75